ANIMAL EMOTIONS

Fig. 1. Hieronymus Bosch, Ship of Fools (1490–1500)

Christian Montag
with Kenneth L. Davis

ANIMAL EMOTIONS

HOW THEY DRIVE HUMAN BEHAVIOR

Brainstorm Books
Santa Barbara, California

brainstorm books

First published in 2020 by Brainstorm Books
An imprint of punctum books, Earth, Milky Way
https://www.punctumbooks.com

ISBN-13: 978-1-950192-90-8 (print)
ISBN-13: 978-1-950192-91-5 (ePDF)

DOI: 10.21983/P3.305.1.00

LCCN: 2020939596
Library of Congress Cataloging Data is available from the Library of
Congress

Copyediting: Jessica Powell
Book design: Vincent W.J. van Gerven Oei
Cover image: Emir Filipović, Cat paw pints on a medieval manuscript
(close up). July 5, 2011.

Contents

In memory of Jaak Panksepp (1943–2017)

Preface

I am writing these words shortly after hearing of Jaak's death. He was a great colleague and a wonderful, inspiring human. I feel very sad because I have lost a friend. That said, I can't claim to have been extremely close to Jaak. Yet I do not want to make our friendship seem less important than it was. We had a friendship conducted through written correspondence over the course of several years. We discussed not only scientific matters via e-mail, but also exchanged opinions on daily politics (he was a strong democrat), and we e-mailed from time to time about our joys and sorrows. Toward the end, I followed with great sadness Jaak's e-reports about his mounting pain due to his third bout with cancer.

I first came to know Jaak in 2004, when my friend and PhD advisor, Martin Reuter, introduced me to him. I was still a psychology student back then and had recently begun studying Jaak's Affective Neuroscience theory (AN theory). It was nearly eight years after the time of this first meeting that Jaak and I began corresponding regularly via e-mail. Our relationship intensified after we met in the U.S., after Jaak asked to read one of my papers in 2012. I closed my e-mail reply with "warm wishes from Seattle" and happily attached my work. My wife, Susanne, happened to be working in Seattle at that time, but I was not aware that Jaak was living "close by" (some five or six hours) until Susanne and I received an immediate invitation to his home. That's how Jaak was! Susanne and I visited him and his wife, Anesa Miller, in Pullman, Washington, driving through the Palouse with country radio turned up loud, making our way eventually to Yellowstone National Park. I still remember the beautiful sight of the rolling hills surrounding us. These have also been nicely described in Anesa's book, *To Boldly Go* (Miller 2013). What followed our long drive through Washington State was a wonderful evening with Anesa and Jaak at their wooden house. We had a nice meal at a nearby place with a view and a long chat afterwards on their veranda. After this evening, Jaak and I intensified our scientific collaboration, resulting in a series of papers we co-authored, including what was perhaps the last paper he ever wrote, published in April of 2017.[1]

Long story short, Jaak agreed in October 2016 to write the present short volume with me in order to offer an easy and accessible introduction to his theory for non-scientists. As he put it in an e-mail exchange with me dated October 28th, 2016: "In any case, clearly, a readable synoptic AN book is needed rather than another 'fat' one." So, this became our plan.

Aside from this scope, the present text is also an extension of his earlier work, because new topics are included in the present volume that were not initially covered in his great works, *Affective Neuroscience* (Panksepp 1998) and *The Archaeology of Mind* (Panksepp and Biven 2012). To some extent, these new topics also mirror my own work based on Jaak's theory, though I emphasize that Jaak's extremely well-written and accessible books are the real stuff to read. As already mentioned, this present volume is meant only as a small introduction to his work and offers a review of several studies that we worked on together in the last years of his life (all published after his last major book in 2012[2]).

I am aware that, given their length, many readers do not find the time to read Jaak's original works, so my hope is that the present book will serve as a good entry point into the world of Jaak Panksepp. This scope has natural limitations, because

[1] While my group published papers with Jaak's name on the author line after this 2017 paper, these were actually written prior to that date.

[2] Note that his last book, *The Emotional Foundations of Personality: A Neurobiological and Evolutionary Approach,* written with Kenneth L. Davis, who also co-authors this book, was published in 2018, after Jaak's death.

many other relevant theories of emotion exist that illuminate different aspects of our emotional lives. In acknowledgement of this, I have included the last chapter in this volume, which briefly discusses AN theory in the context of other important theories of emotion.

I am very sad that the present volume could not be finished with Jaak. Indeed, the entire book was written without Jaak. But, sometimes, sad events also bring happy moments. In this case, I attended a memorial at a conference in London to honor Jaak's work and got to know Jaak's close friend Kenneth L. Davis, who also co-developed the *Affective Neuroscience Personality Scales* and co-authored *The Emotional Foundations of Personality* with Jaak (Davis and Panksepp 2018). I am so pleased that Ken invested so much time and energy in this book. He not only worked on my first draft, but also extended the book and made valuable additions. Thank you so much, Kenneth, for your tremendous support. I am sure Jaak is delighted about our collaboration.

A word on the perspective presented in this book: in most instances, Ken and I write as "we." Deviations from this can be seen in the personal reports that use a short episode from my life as an illustration of each primary emotional system. Further exceptions are explicitly mentioned in the text.

Finally, a German-language version of this book will hopefully follow in the future, as this was also part of my initial plan with Jaak.

I end this preface (as I think of him) with a phrase Jaak often used to close his emails: "With smiles." And so, to my dear readers: With smiles, Christian.

1

Jaak Panksepp Discovered Seven Ancient Emotions in the Mammalian Brain

"We can actually turn on emotions by stimulating specific areas of the brain. [...] When we turn on an emotion, does the animal feel good or bad? The animal can give us that answer, because it can turn on the stimulation – given a chance – or it can turn it off and that is our measure of feelings."
— Panksepp (2014)

"An emotion is composed of (1) neurochemical processes, (2) expressive behavior, and (3) a subjective experience or feeling state."
Ackerman, Abe, and Izard (1998, 86)

We would add a fourth element to this list: "altered perceptions/thoughts."

What would our lives be without emotions? Our lives would be shallow and boring, nothing would ever be exciting. There would simply be no ups and downs. Our lives would very much resemble a flat line. Imagine you did not know grief or pain; could you then experience a state of pure joy? Without emotions, would your heart jump when the first warm days of spring come or when you see a person you love? Would you be able to experience the psychic impact of music at a concert hall or of the roaring fans in the soccer stadium? Clearly, these kinds of experiences all rely on emotional responses in our brains (and bodies), which make our lives often delightful, but sometimes also very painful. It is not an exaggeration to state that emotions are the fuel of our lives.

Usually, our emotions are strongly controlled. Therefore, we seldom experience situations of raw affect, where emotions simply overwhelm us. This is basically a good thing, because controlling our ancestral emotional urges helps us to respond more appropriately to most of the daily situational demands of our modern society. It is simply not acceptable to always show an emotional response in every given situation. But, from time to time, there are events that can derail us, and we might exhibit something close to raw affect. To illustrate the different strengths and visibility of our operating emotional systems in everyday life, let's consider two situations with different levels of emotional regulation.

In the first scenario, imagine yourself talking with a colleague at work and you hear that they got a promotion you also wanted. Hearing about the promotion is accompanied by an unpleasant angry feeling. You begin to feel your heart pumping faster and a pit in your stomach. As you register these unpleasant sensations, you become aware that you are angry and envious and that you think your colleague's promotion is not fair. You did a much better job! For a moment you are stunned. Nevertheless, you control your emotions so that they are not outwardly visible to others.

In the second scenario, imagine that a close friend or family member has died. You are sitting in front of the computer; the desk is piled with work and you are flooded with grief. You are shaken; you simply feel bad. You can't concentrate and it's impossible to work. You feel so miserable that you begin crying, an outwardly visible expression of your emotion.

In both examples, an external situation of evolutionary significance activated "built-in" (strongly genetically anchored) distinct emotional systems, triggering a raw emotion without further need for cognitive labeling (or construction of an emotion). In the context of the first example, where your colleague got a promotion, you were passed over for the opportunity to receive a limited resource, resulting in angry, envious feelings. In the early times of our species, *Homo sapiens* and their ancestors, this anger response could have led you to fight for at least part of the prey. Your emotional, angry, combative response could have meant that crucial resources would have been at least partly available for you and your own kin. The second example, losing a close friend or family member, represents a significant evolutionary event, because humans are social mammals. Being alone represented a dangerous state in former times, because humans survive better in groups, especially when facing dangerous situations. This is still true today, because clearly, it's easier to get through life with a partner on whom we can rely. Therefore, feeling sad represents an adaptive response to signal the need for help from one's own social network.

Before we learn more about the aforementioned evolution-arily significant scenarios and our emotional heritage, we ask the question: How do we manage to overrule the emotional urges that are triggered by the activity of built-in emotional systems relevant to our survival? Why do our genetic programs seldom overwhelm us (although they are clearly active and influence our behavior)? Remember that in the office example no overt, angry, aggressive response was visible.

First of all, not every situation in our lives triggers our ancient emotional neural circuits so strongly that it results in a full-blown emotional response. We believe that the higher the evolutionary significance of a situation, the stronger the activity of our primal emotional brain systems will be, making it more likely to see a basic emotional response pattern. Aside from this, as complex creatures with "built-in" emotional systems, we are able to rely in many situations more typical of our modern society on the more recently developed ("recently" refers to an evolutionary perspec-tive) cortical "thinking cap" in our brains. This new brain area (the neocortex) enables us to control and regulate ancient brain regions where raw affects can be triggered. This is illustrated by the simple sketch in Figure 1.1, which shows the different evolu-tionary layers of our human brain. This sketch is based on the work of Paul MacLean and is well known in the literature as the Triune Brain Concept (MacLean 1990).[1] Whereas both our neural

[1] For recent arguments against the Triune Brain Concept, see Cesario,

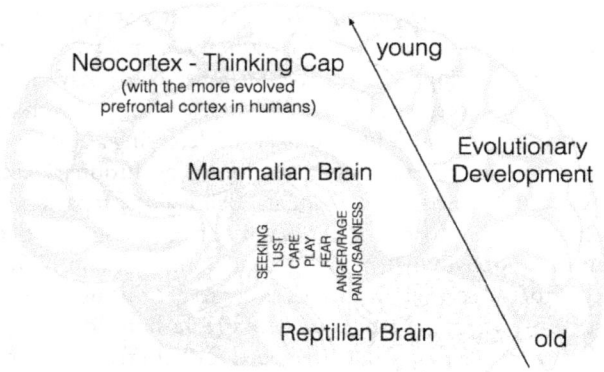

Fig. 1.1 MacLean's Triune Brain Concept and Panksepp's primal emotions.

circuitries for basic bodily functions (such as breathing) as well as those related to our primary emotions reside in the oldest layers, the reptilian and mammalian brains, the evolutionarily youngest layer enables us to reason and also to control and regulate activity in the evolutionarily older layers in a top-down fashion. As one can also derive from the terms "reptilian" and "mammalian" brains, we share many structures of the reptilian brain with the brains of reptiles and many structures of the mammalian brain with the brains of our fellow mammals. While MacLean's concept is currently out of fashion, it still provides a useful heuristic. For example, the reptilian brain (including fish) does not have the emotional capacity to exhibit all seven of Panksepp's primary emotions. Fish exhibit SEEKING, ANGER, and FEAR behavior but lack the social emotions of CARE, SADNESS, and PLAY. There are isolated cases of what one might call the "hint" of CAREing behavior in fish, but fish and reptiles in general do not care for their young. Females of these species typically deposit their eggs in crude nests, and the hatchlings emerge on their own to survive as best they can. Nor do fish or reptiles exhibit social bonding or

Johnson, and Eisthen (2019).

social play. The mammalian emotions CARE, PANIC/SADNESS,[2] and PLAY are the additional genetically endowed capacities that created social mammals and their family structure. In short, due to the homologies observed in these ancient brain layers across species, at the "bottom of our minds" humans have emotional capacities very much like other animals, but at the "top of our minds" we are very different. However, as alluded to above, MacLean's view has often been marginalized because of more recent anatomical evidence and criticized by those who reject an evolved subcortical conception of primary emotions because it offers an oversimplified suggestion that emotions only reside/ arise in the evolutionarily oldest areas of the brain. We argue that this is true for animal emotions, that is, the rawest forms of affect/instinct. But, as we will outline later in this book, there are also more complex derived emotions (such as shame), which are clearly fueled by ancestral emotional energy, and which also rely on the activity of the neocortex and result in more complex emotions. Finally, this sketch suggests that non-human mammals do not have a neocortex. This also is not true, because mammals and *Homo sapiens* possess a neocortex, but in prefrontal areas it is simply not as highly developed in non-human mammals as it is in humans (Donahue et al. 2018; Teffer and Sememdeferi 2012). Indeed, as was discovered by researchers at the Max Planck Institute, a single evolutionarily recent gene mutation (existing only in humans, Neanderthals, and Denisovans, but not in chimpanzees) seems to have resulted in a significant increase in the human neocortex, likely providing a distinct adaptive advantage. This finding supports the evolutionary uniqueness of the human neocortex compared to other mammals (Florio et al. 2015). So, despite limitations, for reasons of (simple) illustration we still like this sketch, because it gives some easy insights into brain evolution, which helps to understand some key arguments of the present work, in particular the concepts of top-down and bottom-up processes, including the more evolved prefrontal cortex in humans.

---

2   Please note that PANIC was Jaak's original term for this emotional system, which is now often used interchangeably with SADNESS.

As we will learn from Jaak's work, we share at least seven primary emotions with our fellow mammalian brothers and sisters and, at the bottom of our minds, we very likely experience feelings similar to those other animals experience (Panksepp 1998). Nevertheless, there are notable differences, because animals feel rather more raw emotions, whereas emotional urges arising from the neural emotional circuitries are comparably more controlled in humans. We say "comparably more controlled," because in extreme situations we can all be overwhelmed by our emotions, by our ancient genetic programs, no matter how strongly our cognitive "thinking cap" tries to regulate the ancient energies of our minds. Emotional activity in these old brain layers can be triggered by events that were of high importance for our ancestors in their long evolutionary development towards *Homo sapiens.* As an illustration: if we experience the loss of a loved one, we can do nothing but feel terrible psychic pain due to the activation of our SADNESS system. In contrast, the inactivation of our SADNESS system, such as when we are with our loved ones and being taken CARE of, simply feels very good. These two cases show some of the painful and pleasant emotional experiences that make us social animals and provide for social bonding. As mentioned, primary emotions are built-in systems in our brains, they are genetically rooted in us; we do not have to learn the reaction patterns accompanying activity in these neural circuits of our animal emotions. In the case of SADNESS, such a reaction pattern could trigger the production of distress vocalizations (crying behavior) to attract the attention of the caregiver.[3]

Before we move on, we would like to briefly summarize Jaak's definition of a primary emotion. In order to speak of a primary emotion (animal or mammalian emotion), the following points need to be observed (Panksepp 2010):

- Primary emotions generate characteristic behavioral-instinctual action patterns;
- They are initially activated by a limited set of unconditional stimuli;

3 For more detailed illustrations of the SADNESS emotion, see the chapter on animal emotions and mental disorders.

- The resulting arousals outlast precipitating circumstances.
- Emotional arousals gate/regulate various sensory inputs into the brain;
- They control learning and help program higher brain cognitive activities;
- With maturation, higher brain mechanisms come to regulate emotional arousals.

In order to illustrate this complex definition, we would like to give an example regarding the emotion of FEAR. Imagine that while hiking through a beautiful national park, you stumble upon a snake. As snakes were dangerous for humans over a long evolutionary process, the sight of the snake alone can trigger an in-born FEAR response in our brains; hence the snake is an unconditional stimulus eliciting a behavioral-instinctual action pattern. By activity of the FEAR system, our body is then set into arousal. Energy is pumped through our body to provide us with enough power to fight the enemy or maybe, in this case, to flee from the scene to avoid an attack by the snake. Even if you successfully escaped this dangerous situation, it might take a short while until you have your senses together and calm down (this is the arousal outlasting precipitating circumstances). Notably, the FEAR circuit can also be elicited by conditioned stimuli, but this requires first learning to associate a certain stimulus with danger. This is possible, as we will see, by linking activities of primary emotional systems with those from higher anatomical areas of the brain.

Like all mammals, humans strive to reduce bad feelings and to increase the occurrence of episodes of good feelings. For example, feeling SAD signals a loss of support and, as a consequence, the individual searches for help in one's own social network. *Homo sapiens* are simply stronger in groups than we are alone and when we feel alone, we need to be taken care of. Moreover, our built-in genetic primary emotional systems make social interactions rewarding: how good it feels when we are cared for in situations of loneliness! In particular, this feels good via contact comfort, meaning when a relative, good friend, or partner embraces us.

Through experiencing good or bad feelings, primary emotions help us to learn as they guide our lives. If a child has touched a hot oven, they will not do it again, out of FEAR of feeling that awful pain again. The oven was so hot, and the pain so strong! As one can see from this example, our emotions are also linked to our memories. Feeling diverse emotions is so important because if something feels good, we're likely to behave in the same way in the future, in order to feel that good again. Feeling good is simply very rewarding. If something feels bad, we try to modify our behavior so as not to experience that awful feeling again. Feeling bad feels like a punishment to us. Notably, abundant research has demonstrated that emotional memories, in particular, are the ones that end up sticking like glue in our brains (Alberini 2010).

Due to the groundbreaking work of Jaak Panksepp, we know that at the bottom of our minds we share with other mammals four sources of positive affect, such as emotional joy/pleasure, and three sources of negative affects, all of which guide our lives. Among Jaak's many lifetime achievements is the detailed mapping of the neural circuitry underlying these primal emotions by means of electrical brain stimulation. Please see Table 1.1 for the exact neuroanatomical areas underlying the seven innate emotional systems. In this table, one can also see which neurotransmitters/neuropeptides (important molecules in the communication between nerve-cells (neurons)) enable the information flux in these brain areas, ultimately leading us to feel an emotion. As this book is written for non-scientists, we will not go into greater detail about Table 1.1, but include it for interested readers.[4] Crucially, Jaak demonstrated that inserting an electrode in brain areas presented in Table 1.1, together with stimulating these brain areas with electric current, leads to a characteristic emotional behavioral action pattern, often accompanied by an emotional sound typical of that animal. For example, stimulating parts of the so-called medial forebrain bundle (a brain structure underlying the SEEKING system) results in an enthusiastic exploration of the animal's environment. Jaak also showed that PLAY behavior in rats is accompanied by 50kHz chirps, which, in many respects, resembles human laughter. As these chirps

4   We have written extensively elsewhere about the use of this table in
    guiding neuroscientific research. See, for example, Montag and Davis
    (2018); Montag and Panksepp (2016; 2017).

are ultrasonic and, therefore, inaudible to the human ear, Jaak and his colleagues needed to use special equipment to register these vocalizations. This was among Jaak's most famous discoveries, and earned him the nickname "Rat Tickler" (Langer 2017), because rats also reacted with these ultrasonic chirps when being tickled by Jaak (Burgdorf, Panksepp, and Moskal 2011; Panksepp and Burgdorf 2000). See how similar rats and humans are! If small children play (or are tickled), they also laugh out loud with pure joy. With respect to the aforementioned electrical brain stimulation, it should be mentioned that this method is also used in human brain surgery procedures. Here it has been observed that externally triggering certain brain areas in humans can lead to involuntary laughter or crying (Krack et al. 2001; Caruana et al. 2020). Of course, this was not the research objective of those studies, but rather, these results were observed incidentally when conducting brain surgery. Nevertheless, these results strongly underline the similarities between humans and other mammals at the bottom of our minds.

As already mentioned, Jaak carved out seven primary emotional systems, which we also call in this book "animal emotions" (as they can all be observed in all mammals, including humans; and some also in evolutionarily older animals, as described earlier). On the bright side of affect, Jaak registered SEEKING, LUST, CARE, and PLAY. We have already briefly introduced SEEKING. Activity in this area is accompanied by feelings of energy and enthusiasm and results in explorative behavior. SEEKING activity provides us with energy in the search for food, or a mate, but also gives us energy for other everyday life activities. Note that SEEKING activity may be lacking in cases of full-blown depression.[5] The LUST and CARE systems are deeply entwined, with the LUST system presenting as evolutionarily older, because evolution first needed to design a system for reproduction and then a system for bringing up children (CAREing for them). CARE activities also promote bonding with others and promote satisfying and lasting relationships. One of the most important hormones of this system is oxytocin (often and much too simplistically called the "love hormone"), which is secreted when we

5   See also Chapter 3.

are being cared for.[6] Notably, when we feel SAD, human touch helps to regulate and reduce SADNESS activity by producing oxytocin in our brains. Finally, we all have a built-in PLAY system. Unfortunately, this still represents an understudied emotion, but it is clear that all mammals play, particularly at young ages. As we will discuss in a later chapter, PLAY is an important means through which children learn social competencies and motor skills.

On the dark side of emotions, Jaak mapped the FEAR, RAGE/ANGER, and SADNESS systems. FEAR activity is triggered in situations of danger and results in a genetically programmed fight, flight, or freezing reaction. The appropriate FEAR reaction depends, among other factors, on the concept of defensive distance. If, for instance, a predator is relatively far away, mild FEAR may be experienced but little action will result. When danger is near, we freeze or flee for our lives. Many predators react to movement, thus in certain dangerous situations, freezing can make you "invisible" to the eye of the predator. Just think of the famous T-Rex scene in the blockbuster movie *Jurassic Park,* in which T-Rex is closing in on Dr. Grant, who freezes in order to avoid detection. When freezing or escape is not possible, mammals will vigorously fight for their lives, in which case FEAR is also fueled by RAGE energy.

The RAGE/ANGER system is a bit more complicated to understand. Being frustrated can trigger it, which could be a consequence of not getting a reward. Imagine that you studied extremely hard for a final exam, but you fail and are the only person to fail the course. Your classmates are making fun of you. Clearly, this would result in ANGER activity, too often also accompanied by overt aggressive behavior. In the animal world, ANGER reactions are often a result of territorial conflict or arise from the need to protect offspring from dangerous predators. As earlier outlined, it also developed in order to fight for limited resources. Another trigger for the ANGER system can be bodily restraint, which could be the case when in the clutches of a predator, as alluded to in the previous paragraph.

6 Originally, oxytocin was only known for its function in maternal labor and lactation.

This emotion – along with the other primary emotions - can even be observed in "ordinary" (and evolutionarily insignificant) places such as a soccer stadium. One of the authors (CM) is an enthusiastic fan of his home soccer team – I. FC Köln. In particular when derby-games are going on (which means that teams from neighboring towns are playing against each other), some fans react to a defeat with strong ANGER, sadly, from time to time, also accompanied by verbal and bodily aggression. This is somewhat surprising because the personal lives of these "fans" do not generally depend on the outcome of the game (aside from cases in which people bet money on a game, etc.). This example shows that the simple identification with a soccer team is able to produce relatively raw affects, even in situations that are not really important for the personal life of an individual. Whether the home-team wins or loses does not at all change the fan's personal family life or professional career! This example nicely illustrates that activity in primary emotions can be linked to activity of higher brain layers when it is triggered by learned concepts. Hence, activity in primary emotions can also be elicited by events beyond the unconditional stimuli that are relevant from an evolutionary point of view. In this case, learning has clearly taken place, as energy in neural circuits underlying primary emotions has become associated with events from everyday life.

The last primal emotion to be named (again) is SADNESS. SADNESS activity is triggered by losing contact with loved ones, which results in separation distress. This will be illustrated, beyond what has been mentioned above, in more detail in the chapter on mental disorders.

How do we feel when each positive and negative primal emotion is triggered? In Table 1.1, we present the straightforward terms presented in Jaak's TED Talk. In addition, we note that emotions preceded language and language can only approximate a description of an actual emotional experience.

At the end of the present chapter, we will also summarize why the primary emotional systems have been conserved in the mammalian brain. In order to do so, we will consider the question from the perspective of an evolutionary biologist asking what selective advantages go along with "owning" each of the built-in emotional systems. The SEEKING system provides mammals with psychological "energy" (i.e., enthusiasm) to explore the environment. This is necessary for finding a mate as well as food to nourish both brain and body. LUST is the driving force behind the biological urge to transfer one's own genome (and hence also that of the species, *Homo sapiens*) to offspring of the next generation. As described earlier, LUST and CARE circuitries overlap to some extent, which makes sense, as neural circuits for sexual reproduction must have evolved before a genetic program to take care of the offspring. The CARE emotion reflects the simple fact that humans are social mammals and it ensures that parents care for their offspring so that young children will grow into adults and, in turn, have their own families. PLAY behavior is important for learning social competencies and motor skills. Such skills help us to get along better in complex social groups as adults.

Without a FEAR response (along with the learning it promotes) *Homo sapiens* would not have optimal abilities to escape and avoid dangerous situations and to carefully monitor the safety of their environments. Activity of the ANGER/RAGE system is observed when mammals are required to defend their resources or themselves, as when trapped by a predator, but also in situations of frustration, when an expected reward is absent or taken away. RAGE activity may also arise in mammals as a means of resolving territorial conflicts. PANIC/SADNESS reflects separation distress and signals a situation of having lost contact with an important person or of being lost. As *Homo sapiens* are social animals, separation from a caregiver or another important person triggers a distress reaction leading to distress vocalization (crying in young children) to signal the urgent need to reunite with a partner or a parent. Ultimately, as with CARE, *Homo sapiens* are more secure in groups than alone. So, it comes as no surprise that CARE activity can counteract and regulate SADNESS arousal.

Before closing this chapter, there are two more important thoughts to share. As we have noted, Jaak Panksepp discovered seven primary emotions driving mammalian behavior in a bottom-up fashion. To understand the term "bottom-up," we refer again to Figure 1.1, depicting Paul MacLean's sketch of the Triune Brain Concept. There may be other as-yet unmapped primal emotions, such as DOMINANCE (van der Westhuizen and Solms 2015), to be included in future lists, though social dominance urges are likely to arise from the interplay of several primary-process emotional systems. Only the future will tell if more primal raw animal emotions need to be added to the seven well-known ones mentioned in Table 1.1. Finally, some readers will ask themselves where to put "emotions" like shame, guilt, or surprise (the latter can be seen as a unique expression in human faces). In the present volume we are focusing on raw, but mighty animal emotions. Emotions such as shame or guilt arise from a complex interaction of activity of primal emotions located at the bottom of our minds mingling with activity from evolutionarily newer areas such as the neocortex. Both shame and guilt are likely fueled bottom-up by SADNESS energy (you feel SAD about not having lived up to your aspirations in front of others). Thus, shame and guilt are more "cognitive" emotions, whereas with respect to pure or raw SADNESS activity, the genetic program is in full operation. When this neural circuit is active, humans are overwhelmed by despair and grief.

A last word on surprise: the case of this facial expression has been much disputed over the years. Some research suggests that surprise is not an emotion at all, because you can also be surprised about a "surprising" non-emotional fact: Did you know that in Beijing alone about 90,000 cars were registered in 2016? This fact might cause a surprise reaction in you without being "colored" by a certain emotion. But, as always, there are exceptions to the rule. Perhaps you are an environmental activist and you will rage about this unbelievable number. In any case, surprise is likely not a primal emotion and feelings of shame/guilt seem to be fueled by both subcortical and cortical energy.

Table 1.1 is taken from Montag and Panksepp (2017) with an update from Jaak's TED Talk:

Panksepp's primary emotional systems and the accompanying feelings mentioned in brackets	Brain neuro-anatomy related to these primary emotional systems	Some key neuropeptides / neurotransmitters that modulate the primary emotional systems
FEAR (anxious)	Central and lateral Amygdala to medial Hypothalamus and dorsal Periaqueductal Gray (PAG)	Glutamate (+), DBI(+), CRF (+), CCK (+), Alpha-MSH (+), Oxytocin (−)
ANGER/RAGE (angry)	Medial Amygdala to Bed Nucleus of Stria Terminalis (BNST). Medial and perifornical Hypothalamus to PAG	Substance P (+), Ach (+), Glutamate (+)
PANIC/SADNESS (lonely & sad)	Anterior Cingulate, BNST and Preoptic Area, dorsome-dial Thalamus, PAG	Opioids (−), Oxytocin (−), Prolactin (−), CRF (+), Glutamate (+)
SEEKING (enthusiastic)	Nucleus Accumbens – Ventral Tegmental Area (VTA), mesolimbic and mesocortical Outputs, lateral Hypothalamus to PAG	Dopamine (+), Glutamate (+), Opioids (+), Neurotensin (+), Orexin (+)

CARE (tender & loving)	Anterior Cingulate, BNST, Preoptic Area, VTA, PAG	Oxytocin (+), Prolactin (+), Dopamine (+), Opioids (+/–)
LUST (horny)	Cortico-medial Amygdala, BNST, Preoptic Hypothalamus, ventromedial Hypothalamus, PAG	Gonadal steroids (+), Vasopressin (+ male), Oxytocin (+ female), LH-RH (+)
PLAY (joyous)	Dorso-medial Diencephalon, Parafascicular Area, PAG	Opioids (+/–), Glutamate (+), Ach (+), Endocannabinoids

Table 1.1. + = Excitatory effects / – = inhibiting effects; DBI = diazepam binding inhibitor; CRF = corticotropin releasing factor/ hormone; CCK = cholecystokinin; alpha-MSH = alpha melanocyte stimulating hormone; Ach = acetylcholine; LH-RH = luteinizing hormone releasing hormone.

All systems are controlled by glutamate in an excitatory way and GABA in an inhibitory way. Also, the global state control systems, namely brainstem norepinephrine and serotonin systems that ascend throughout higher brain regions, tend to excite and inhibit, respectively, all of the primal emotional systems as well as waking/ arousal and sleep/relaxation states. This table should be seen as work in progress.

Summary

Jaak Panksepp discovered seven built-in primary emotional systems, which influence our behavior bottom-up from ancient brain layers. The term "built-in" means that these primary emotional systems have a strong heritable component, otherwise they would not be homologous conserved across species. One of Jaak's main research methods represented the technique of electrical brain stimulation. Thereby, he investigated which brain areas need to be triggered to elicit a distinct emotional response. According to his work, we can observe four circuitries for positive emotions called SEEKING, LUST, CARE, and PLAY. Moreover, there are three circuitries for negative emotions called FEAR, ANGER/RAGE, and SADNESS. Each primary emotion represents a tool for survival, enabling survival of the individual and/or the species. All primal emotions are written in smallcaps to distinguish their use as scientific labels and in order not to confuse them with the typical lower-case terms used in the psychological literature or by people discussing emotions in a general way.

SEEKING

The sun was shining through the window and I slowly opened my eyes. The last fragments of a dream were passing by and then were quickly gone. I could not remember the dream's content, but it seemed not to have been a bad one. I felt no emotional turmoil, I just felt good. It was one of my first nights in Lanarka on Cyprus and I was starting to relax after the first few days of vacation. It usually takes some time for me to adjust to holiday time without feeling the urge to work. This morning, my work was far away. Through the open window, I could hear the waves of the Mediterranean Sea. I got out of bed, stretched my arms towards the ceiling and turned towards the window. Through the windows, I could see the glistening sea, where the sun reflected in diamond-like waves. Above this, the sky shimmered in a perfect blue. I felt fresh and full of energy. This energy was not directed at anything, but I knew that I could spend my whole day exploring the island of Cyprus.

2

Animal Emotions and Human Personality

> "Jeder Jeck ist anders."
> Loosely translated into English:
> "Everyone is peculiar in their own way."
> — Saying from Cologne

The study of human personality is as old as mankind and can be traced back to Galen,[1] who postulated early ideas about potential links between bodily fluids and the four temperament types famously known as melancholic, sanguine, choleric, and phlegmatic. Galen's ideas are noteworthy because he was already making a case for a biological investigation of human personality right from the start of the human quest to understand why we are the creatures we are. Understanding human personality and questions such as "Why I am the kind of person that I am?" is of great scientific interest far beyond human curiosity. It has been well documented that personality is linked to many important variables such as life satisfaction, well-being, job performance, longevity, and health behavior as well as, perhaps most importantly, to one's likelihood of suffering from mental disorders.[2]

1 Galen of Pergamon was a physician living around 129–217 CE.
2 Here the personality dimension of Neuroticism has been strongly linked to suffering from depression or anxiety disorders; see below for further explanation.

Please see also Christian's book on personality (Montag 2016) or Ken and Jaak's recent work (Davis and Panksepp 2018).

Personality can be defined as emotional and cognitive patterns resulting in predictably stable behavioral action tendencies. The issue of stability has been discussed in two areas, namely time stability over the life course and situational stability. Longitudinal studies have demonstrated that personality tends to be stable over one's lifetime, and a review article by Edmonds et al. (2008) came to the conclusion that, without concentrated effort, you will be in ten years about more or less the same person as you are today. Nevertheless, slight changes in personality are visible over the course of humans' lives and these tend to be positive changes because humans typically become more agreeable and conscientious as they get older.

The second issue with regard to stability concerns stability within the context of different situational demands. This is a fascinating topic because humans do not always behave as consistently as one would expect given a certain personality type; this has been coined the *personality paradox* in the literature. This paradox was explored by the prominent psychologist Walter Mischel (perhaps most famous for his marshmallow experiment with children in which he tested their delay of gratification abilities). He observed that stability of personality has to be described via so called *if–then functions* (Mischel and Shoda 1995). Simply put, this means that if we are facing the same or very similar situations, our behavior seems to grow more consistent, but in different situations, our behavior may vary. Hence, context matters. This could manifest in conscientious behavior at work, but less conscientious behavior at home. For example, my desktop computer at work is always "tidy," but with my domestic work, I am comparably less diligent. Speaking in if–then functions, *if* I am at work, *then* I am conscientious; *if* am doing domestic work, *then* I am less conscientious. Note that higher Conscientiousness usually results in higher Conscientiousness in several areas of one's own life, but to varying degrees.[3] Please see also a recent review dealing with the question how certain life events shape human personality by Bleidorn, Hopwood, and Lucas (2018).

3 We could have used any personality trait as an example here.

The term "personality" can also be illuminated by contrasting the term "trait," describing stable feelings and cognitive/action patterns, with the term "state." The latter describes a more momentary variable describing a person's current state or mood. To illustrate this further, when using a self-report personality questionnaire, one could ask a person to respond to the prompt "In general, I am anxious," which would mirror a trait. If we asked the person to respond to a prompt such as "Right now, I am anxious," this would reflect a state. Of course, the terms "trait" and "state" are to a degree entwined, because an anxious person (trait) should statistically also behave more anxiously in many situations of everyday life (state). Therefore, some researchers have suggested that statistically, the state of a person over a long period of time results in the creation of that person's trait, although this function is far from perfect and both terms – traits and states – have some unique concepts not related to each other.

While personality theory has a long history (often somewhat chaotic and with little consensus), through the statistical analysis of adjectives, personality psychology arrived at a widely accepted solution with five broad traits describing human personality (often simply called the Big Five). These five personality traits – Openness to Experience, Conscientiousness, Extraversion, Agreeableness, and Neuroticism – can be easily remembered with the acronym OCEAN. Openness to Experience describes persons who are open, have high intellect, and a sense of aesthetics. Conscientious persons are diligent and punctual. Extraversion is associated with being socially outgoing, talkative, and assertive. Agreeableness is linked to being a good team player, having high empathic skills, and being a caring person. Finally, Neuroticism is characterized by being more anxious, emotionally unstable (e.g., moody), and depressed. As stated above, higher scores on this last personality trait are linked to a higher risk of suffering from an affective disorder.

These Big Five traits were derived by applying a "lexical" approach, meaning, the attempt to extract personality information embedded in our everyday use of language. Starting in the 1930s and '40s, many researchers (Raymond B. Cattell, Donald W. Fiske, Lewis R. Goldberg – to name a few) used a statistical approach called "factor analysis" to find patterns in thousands of attribute words (mostly adjectives) that we use in everyday life to characterize ourselves and others (McCrae and John 1992; Montag and Elhai 2019). The idea behind this objective approach is a simple one. Personality manifests itself in the language we use on a daily basis. This makes sense, because how often do we describe others by using attribute words (e.g., "Oh, she is such a kind and generous person!")? These statistical analyses of human language led to a replication of a five-factor structure across many diverse cultures.[4]

But an important question is: how do Panksepp's animal emotions provide us a better understanding of human personality? We will discuss this and show specifically how Panksepp's primary emotions link to the Big Five later in the chapter. However, we would first like to revisit the evolutionary perspective from Chapter 1 and consider both Charles Darwin's important works

4 There are exceptions that need to be stated, of which the following is but one example: Openness to Experience has not been robustly observed in China and some personality characteristics strongly related to Confucian culture might only be appropriately covered when administering Chinese personality inventories in China. For a broader discussion and problems in detecting the Big Five beyond Western populations see Laajaj et al. (2019).
    Aside from the robustness of these personality dimensions observed worldwide, we mention that there still exists a discussion among personality psychologists as to how many personality traits are, in fact, needed to describe human personality exhaustively. Here, researchers come to different conclusions, such as three or six dimensions (instead of five). In order to make a long story short, we refer to what has been said by two prominent researchers working in the tradition of the Big Five Model – Paul Costa and Robert McCrae. They argue that the Big Five can be seen as the Christmas tree upon which all other personality traits can be decorated. For example, a person described as high-scoring in the personality trait called Sensation Seeking is both open to experience and highly extraverted. With respect to individual differences in animal emotions, Jaak and Christian saw this Christmas tree metaphor a bit differently, as will be outlined shortly. Aside from this, statistical issues and/or some cultural aspects are, to some extent, responsible for the slight deviations from the most often observed number of five personality traits to describe a human.

on natural selection and also return to Paul MacLean's idea of the Triune Brain Concept. Starting with the latter (and to briefly repeat it), Paul MacLean sketched the human brain in three developmental layers called "reptilian brain," "mammalian brain," and the "neocortex." The reptilian brain represents the evolutionarily oldest parts, followed by the mammalian brain and then our cortical thinking cap, the neocortex. If one seeks to find an answer about which part of human personality is evolutionarily oldest, Jaak's work helps to find an answer, because the neural circuitry harboring our ancient animal emotions in the human brain are located in both the reptilian and mammalian areas of the brain. If we return to the assertion that personality manifests itself in stable emotional, motivational, and cognitive patterns, clearly, individual differences in emotional/motivational aspects must be evolutionarily oldest (as they are located in the most ancient areas of the human brain).

We turn now to Charles Darwin. He developed his groundbreaking ideas from the natural observations he made during his world tour aboard a ship called the *Beagle,* a journey that included a famous stop on the Galapagos Archipelago, where he stumbled on what are now called Darwin finches. In observing these birds, it came to his attention that finches with different beak sizes existed and that these different beak sizes could be linked to different islands. Variation in the finches' beak sizes resulted from different evolutionary pressures on each island which, in turn, favored different beak sizes. On islands with small and soft food, small beak sizes are preferable, while on islands with large and hard-to-crack seeds, large beak sizes are better adapted. It has been observed that these finches that better adapted to their island also produced more offspring.

Importantly, some variation in the finches' beak size could still be observed on each island, which can be explained by the concept of *fluctuation selection*: if a drought occurs on an island, the food availability could change and favor those with large beaks, because the small, soft seeds are not available anymore. Hence, variation of the trait *beak size* supported the species' survival. This concept has been adapted to personality psychology by David Nettle with so called trade-off models. He argues in a paper (Nettle 2006) and a follow-up book (Nettle 2009)

37

that variation in personality can best be understood in terms of the natural selection processes put forward by Darwin. Every personality type comes with costs and benefits depending on the environment a person lives in. For every human, this ultimately suggests searching for an environment that fits particularly well with one's own personality type (because it is much harder to change one's own personality than one's environment). This process can be observed in growing children and adolescents when, as they become more independent of their parents, they start to select environments that are more suited to their own genotype and personality (Scarr and McCartney 1983). To illustrate the aforementioned costs and benefits of distinct personality traits in different environments, Nettle has demonstrated that extraverts have advantages in life, because they have easier access to the other sex and hence they also tend to have statistically more children. In contrast, they are more prone to accidents, because they tend to exhibit riskier behavior and end up statistically more often in hospitals. See! It is not simply good or bad to be extraverted.

Considering another personality type, it is well known that neurotic persons are more prone to suffer from an affective disorder such as depression. On the other hand, they remain safer in uncertain or even dangerous situations (as they more carefully monitor the environment). In sum, personality is not good or bad per se, but the success of one's own unique Big Five personality constellation depends on the environmental niche a person is living in. Again, how does knowledge about ancient animal emotions enlarge this picture to better understand why variation in personality still occurs in the human population?

For one answer to this question we have to turn briefly to statistics. Like many things in nature once they are measured, these personality dimensions tend to be "normally distributed." This means that the majority of people in a population have moderate scores on a personality trait such as Extraversion, with only a few people being characterized by extremely low or high scores (resulting, for example, in a more introverted or extraverted personality). Nevertheless, it is evident that variation in personality occurs, and we are convinced that the observable individual differences in the Big Five traits (with the exception of Conscientiousness) have their foundation in Panksepp's primary emotions and can be explained, to a great extent, by individual differences in these same animal emotions. Such individual differences in animal emotions likely result from individual differences in subcortical neuroanatomical structures and functions resulting from the molecular genetic foundation underlying these ancient animal emotions.

Notably, these ancient neural circuitries are shared in every mammalian being, but the strength with which these animal emotions operate on a daily level depends on the unique underlying neural underpinning of a person's brain, augmented by their individual environments; that is, their individual learning experiences. Hence, we are not speaking of the absence or presence of a primary emotional system (this is not a "1" or "0" function), but rather of the different operating strengths of these systems resulting from an individual's brain architecture interacting with their life experiences. As outlined in the first chapter, animal emotions are *tools for survival* and every organism depends on these systems to adapt successfully to its environment. Nevertheless, in line with Nettle's idea, varying degrees of strength of these emotional systems are of better value in some environments than in others. In accordance with AN theory, we believe that animal emotions are the fuel of Nettle's trade-off model, locating each individual's Big Five personality traits along the aforementioned personality continuum.

This idea is also depicted in Figure 2.1, showing that the unique personality pattern of a person arises from a complex interaction of bottom-up emotional urges (activity of primal emotions) and cortical top-down emotion-regulation strategies.[5]

5   Complicating matters, the activity of each primary emotional system, ergo animal emotion, is a result of both tonic and phasic energy bursts in the underlying neural circuitry. Tonic describes the kind of energy with which the neural circuit underlying an animal emotion usually operates without further stimulation from the environment. But in order to understand the current activation level of a distinct animal emotion, phasic information must also be considered. Thus, the activation level of the neural circuit underlying the animal emotion is also being triggered by an environmental stimulus. To explain this a bit better: an anxious person would be characterized by a higher tonic FEAR circuit, which will be more easily physically activated by a

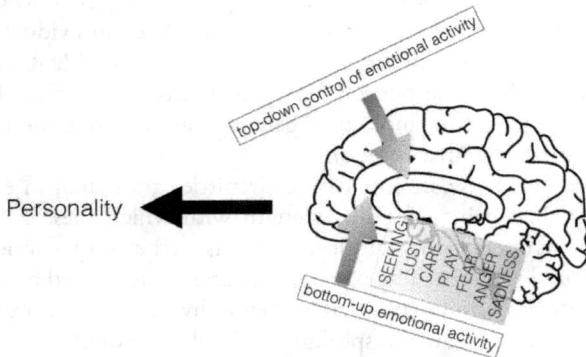

Fig. 2.1 Personality arises from a complex interaction of individual differences in bottom-up emotional urges and top-down (cognitive) emotional regulation abilities. Figure modified from Montag and Panksepp (2017a).

As a result, a person characterized by low Agreeableness might be best described by an overreacting ANGER system, together with less than optimal top-down cognitive brakes. Hence, we could use the metaphor of a bull in a china shop.

Since one of the authors of the present book (KD), Jaak Panksepp, and another of Panksepp's former students, Larry Normansell, published the *Affective Neuroscience Personality Scales* (ANPS) in 2003 to measure the strength of the animal emotions in human personalities (Davis, Panksepp, and Normansell 2003; Davis and Panksepp 2011), many studies have replicated their findings with consistent relationships between the ANPS and the Big Five. In a recent study, Jaak and Christian tried to more broadly answer the question: which primary emotional system/animal emotion underlies each of the Big Five personality traits? In other words, which varying degrees of innate animal emotions in people's brains fuel our complex personalities from

potentially dangerous situation (such as walking home through a dark alleyway), or in light of actual danger (someone is attacking a person in the dark street).

the bottom up? In our work, we assessed individual differences in animal emotions and the Big Five traits and observed robust association patterns in three countries: the U.S., Germany, and China (Montag and Panksepp 2017a). In another paper, we were also able to observe the same associations in persons recruited for our work in Belgrade, Serbia (Montag et al. 2019).[6] Such replication across diverse ethnic/cultural groups (encompassing ten different languages as we write this chapter) speaks for an ancestral global effect. So, what are these consistent (dare we say *universal*?) associations between individual differences in animal emotions as measured by the ANPS and the Big Five?

We confirmed in our data sets that the SEEKING system is likely the evolutionary foundation of Openness to Experience; the PLAY system the foundation of Extraversion; low ANGER and high CAREing the basis for Agreeableness; and finally, high FEAR, SADNESS, ANGER the basis for Neuroticism. As one can see in Figure 2.2, we also included a box with SEEKING below the term Extraversion. In many theories, Extraversion is linked to reward processing (extraverted people might react more strongly to social rewards than introverts), but on this point, our three-country dataset from the U.S., Germany, and China was somewhat inconclusive. This is the reason we put a question mark in the SEEKING box. As a consequence, future research will need to further investigate the relevance of a highly active SEEKING system for being an extraverted person. But also note that AN theory suggests that the SEEKING system energizes all primary emotions.

Importantly, as seen in Figure 2.2, the personality trait of Conscientiousness is not strongly associated with any of the animal emotions. As mentioned previously, our data sets do not consistently show that Conscientiousness has its basis in the ani-

6 Further work resulting from this collaboration by Knežević et al. (2020) associates individual differences in primary emotional systems with the HEXACO model. This model adds to the Big Five a factor called Honesty/Humility (note the X stands for eXtraversion and the rest of the acronym is self-explanatory). We do not want to go into more detail, but leave this footnote for the readers interested in personality psychology.

Big Five of Personality/Five Factor Model of Personality

Openness to Experience	Conscientious-ness	Extraversion	Agreeable-ness	Neuroticism

Primary Emotional Systems influencing the Big Five of Personality

high SEEKING		high PLAY	high CARE	high FEAR
		high SEEKING?	low ANGER	high SADNESS
				high ANGER

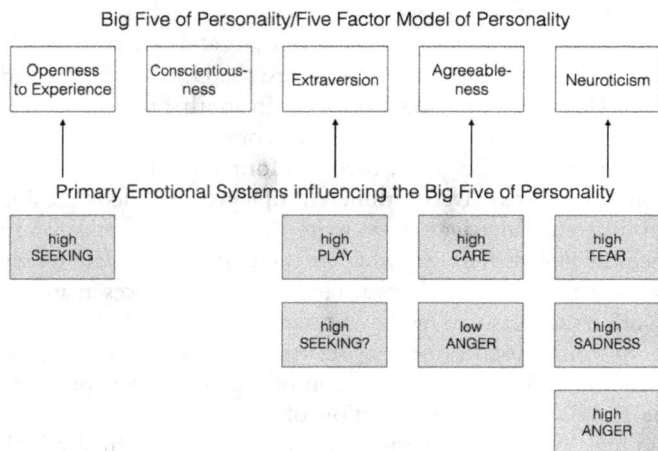

Fig. 2.2 Primary emotional systems influencing human personality bottom-up. Figure modified from Montag and Panksepp (2017).

mal emotions. In fact, Conscientiousness has only been reported in personality studies of higher primates, which is consistent with the idea that Conscientiousness is mostly involved in the top-down regulation of emotions rather than being a primary emotion itself.

As the development of the *Affective Neuroscience Personality Scales* (ANPS and a shorter version called ANPS-AR)[7] to assess individual differences in animal emotions has been based on Panksepp's neuroscientific research findings, our results from the cross-cultural questionnaire research also give an indirect idea about which molecules, brain structures, and functions putatively represent the ancestral parts of the kind of individual

---

7   This inventory has been used to assess primary emotions in the above-mentioned studies. Please find a short version of this question-naire called ANPS-AR, along with norm data from a large data set that you can use for comparison, in the appendix of the present book. The ANPS-AR was originally published by Montag and Davis (2018).

creatures we are (Montag and Panksepp 2017). Again, we refer to Table 1.1, where the molecules and brain regions are described.

To fully understand human personality, we also need to briefly mention the nature–nurture debate, which has been resolved to a large extent. Twin studies suggest that about 50% of individual differences in personality can be accounted for by genetics and the other 50% by the environment.[8] Twin studies follow the idea that if monozygotic twins are more similar than dizygotic twins, genetic influences should play a certain role in individual differences in the behavior or psychological construct under investigation. It's worth noting that this rule of thumb is clearly an oversimplification and there exist many more (complex) models in this large field of research – not presented in this volume – all of which help to disentangle genetic and environmental influences on individual differences in human personality. Going beyond estimating the impact of both nature and nurture on individual differences in human personality, the new field of epigenetic studies demonstrates, on a molecular level, how the environment shapes genetic activity. This means that a genetic disposition for depression does not necessarily mean that a person will suffer from depression or develop a strong neurotic personality type. In contrast, both adverse environmental influences, such as abuse in childhood, together with genomic risk constellations, make it much more likely that such a psychological phenotype develops. This example illustrates the idea of the so-called *inherited stress sensitivity*. Note that other gene–environment interactions can be observed and we have described this complicated issue elsewhere (Montag and Hahn 2018).

The genome holds the blueprint of our human body, including our brain's structure and function. External triggers often influence what kind of information from the genome is provided at a given moment to produce a molecule in our brain. In sum, gene–environment interactions mold into individual differences in brain structure and function (and their ancient animal emotions), ultimately explaining our human personalities in a bottom-up fashion. Given the manifold studies showing correlations between personality and brain structure/function, as

8   See, e.g., the work by Polderman et al. (2015).

assessed with modern brain imaging techniques (e.g., magnetic resonance imaging[9]), together with classic findings from (sad and gruesome) brain lesion cases, we now have extensive evidence that our human personalities arise from our human brains. Despite these advances in understanding what makes us human and the kind of people we are, modern science is still only beginning to understand the complex neural underpinnings of human personality. It is clear that complicated neural networks need to be taken into account to fully understand an individual's personality.[10] Neural network means that wired activity from different brain areas gives rise to the way we are.

We close this section with a last word on the personalities of our fellow mammals. As animal emotions are at the heart of human personality, it is no wonder that: i) individual differences in animal emotions also exist in other mammalian species; and that ii) these differences also speak for the existence of animal personalities. But this is another story to which we will return in Chapter 4.

---

9 See also the review by Markett, Montag, and Reuter (2016).
10 See also a new work on so-called network personality neuroscience by Markett, Montag, and Reuter (2018).

Summary

Human personality is strongly driven by our animal emotions anchored in evolutionarily old layers of our human brains. If we want to understand why we are the creatures we are, we clearly have to start to understand these oldest layers of our brains and how they drive our human behavior.

Variation in human personality still exists, because different personality constellations operate with different success in different environments. This can be nicely illustrated with trade-off models and the process of fluctuation selection as outlined in the present chapter.

LUST

I am strolling through Amsterdam's fantastic Rijksmuseum. The museum is exceptional from an architectural point of view, but perhaps even more so because of its world-famous masterpieces such as Rembrandt's *The Night Watch*.

When visiting the Rijksmuseum it is also well worth one's time to visit side room 2.3 in order to view a (literally) smaller masterpiece (it measures just 18.2 cm × 13.5 cm) called *Mars and Venus Surprised by Vulcan* (1610), by the Dutch painter Joachim Wtewael. It could be seen as a proof of the long human preoccupation with LUST as expressed in art.

The painting depicts the ancient goddess Venus betraying her husband, Vulcan, with Mars – and everyone's watching. It's a classic theme that's been repeated throughout history, even to this day. For an illustration, look no further than the daily scandals in the tabloids.

The small painting at the Rijksmuseum shows the complexities arising from our mammalian LUST circuitry: LUST can be seen as a major source of conflict and power, but also of pleasure. It is a human obsession heavily depicted in the arts and media – from ancient mythology to the new burlesque movement spearheaded by pin-up star Dita von Teese.

The human body is a source of inspiration and pleasure, but sadly too often also a springboard for religious and political fights in the name of morality and decency. The fights about LUST can get bloody, just as in the animal kingdom. I still vividly remember how two male buffalos clashed their massive heads together in a fight over a female buffalo in Lama Valley.

In addition, to all the hypocrites with their double standards: LUST is here to stay and only the acceptance of our in-built neural LUST circuitry as part of our mammalian existence will bring us towards a psychologically healthier society.

With these written words, I perhaps make a mistake by being too cognitive about LUST. It is a powerful emotion, enabling couples to experience pleasure in this moment of utmost intimacy. How does it *feel* when the neural primary emotion of LUST is turned on? As Jaak answered in his TED Talk (2014): "Horny."

3

Animal Emotions and Mental Disorders: Of Depression and Addiction

"Home is where the heart is."
Or, for Christian:
"Home is where the *Dom* is."

Jaak's AN theory has made many important contributions in the field of psychology and neuroscience. Personally, we feel that two contributions are especially noteworthy. First, and this should not be underestimated, Jaak's research provides a strong basis for an understanding of animal emotions and takes the clear position that mammalian animals: i) feel emotions; and ii) that these ancient emotions are to some extent the same emotions that humans feel. We deal with this topic in more detail in Chapter 4. For now, Jaak put it this way: at the bottom of our minds (the evolutionarily oldest layers) we are very similar to our mammalian siblings, but in the top areas of our minds we are very different. In sum, humans are more cognitive creatures (as Jaak put it in his 2014 TED Talk), and the other mammalian animals are more emotional creatures. Aside from making an important point for the existence of animal emotions and how they are anchored in phylogenetically old layers of the human brain, we must, at the same time, recognize that Jaak saw these primary systems being networked throughout the whole brain and becoming emotional brain systems. Thus, the application of AN theory to better understand mental disorders should be highlighted as a special contribution among Jaak's lifetime achievements. Jaak's research demonstrated, in multiple ways, that imbalances in the neural underpinnings of animal emotions are at the core of mental disorders, which can also be nicely illustrated with examples from psychiatry/psychology.

Let's start with the example of depression. Depression is a devastating state of the human mind that afflicts more than 264 million people around the globe (WHO 2020). It is one of the most important factors contributing to mental disabilities in humans. Although depression can come in different forms, the core symptoms underlying depression are loss of interest, a lack of drive/motivation and, of course, strong feelings of negative affect. In its most extreme form, depression can even lead to suicide.

In order to understand depression, we first highlight the primal emotion of SADNESS. Jaak Panksepp initially called the SADNESS system in our brains the PANIC system, and he linked it closely with separation distress (Panksepp and Watt 2011). These characteristic terms have been chosen for good reason, as we will learn from the following example taken from everyday life. Imagine a child is going with mom to the supermarket. Mom runs into a friend in one of the supermarket aisles and has a short chat with her. While mom is talking with her friend, the child looks around in the supermarket (the SEEKING system is activated!) and the child's attention is caught by some sweets a few feet further down the aisle. The inner voice calls the child: GO GET THE SWEETS! Mom, being absorbed in her chat, does not register that her offspring is walking further and further down the aisle. A few moments later, the child has walked into another aisle and finally realizes that mom is out of view. As mom is out of sight, the child starts sobbing and quickly cries out: "Mom, mom, where are you?" In this situation, mild activity of the SADNESS circuit in the child's brain has been triggered because of being separated from mom. If the child turns out not to be successful in finding mom, they will cry louder, finally resulting in PANIC. Louder distress vocalization co-varies with stronger activity of separation-distress kicking in, ergo, we observe high SADNESS activity. Notably, in this early phase of separation-distress, we record both high SEEKING and high SADNESS activity. The child actively searches for mom. This search is driven by feelings of PANIC that mom is not there anymore. If the child is not successful in reuniting with mom, what follows is a depressed state of mind, as the SEEKING activity is attenuated. This down regulation of SEEKING ultimately saves the mammalian organism some energy (which makes sense from an evolutionary point of view),[1] but SADNESS activity remains high.

The same patterns of primal emotional activity can also be observed in adulthood, when romantic partners break off a relationship. Imagine that a girl is breaking up with her boyfriend. If he wants to rescue the relationship, he would be very sad (due to separation-distress caused by the break-up), but he would also try to win her back (high SEEKING activity). If unsuccessful, SEEKING activity would go down and the boy would feel depressed (as only high SADNESS remains). This kind of SEEKING/SADNESS constellation is what can usually also be observed in full-blown depression: low SEEKING (low engagement with life) and high SADNESS activity. This previously studied "depressive" constellation of primal emotions has also been supported in a recent paper published by one of the authors of the present book (CM), along with Katharina Widenhorn-Müller, Jaak Panksepp, and Markus Kiefer, which provided additional evidence with a questionnaire study contrasting depressed patients and healthy controls (Montag et al. 2017). In this paper, we assessed not states of the primal emotions, but traits measured with the ANPS as described in Chapter 2. We were interested to see if certain configurations of higher/lower trait emotionality would characterize the group of depressed patients. Of high relevance is our observation that low SEEKING, high SADNESS (and high FEAR) not only characterized a group of depressed patients when they were contrasted with healthy participants, but also that, in the healthy population, the same associations with depressive tendencies could be observed. This means that persons with lower SEEKING and higher SADNESS (and FEAR) systems are more prone to depressive tendencies than persons with opposite scores on this continuum. The idea

[1]   There is still hope that mom will find the child, right?

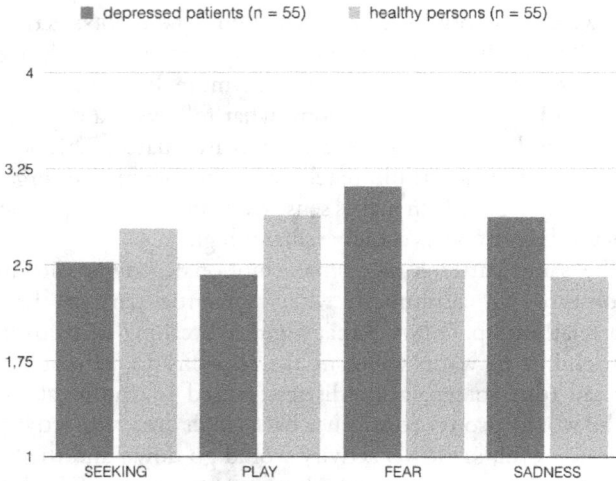

Fig. 3.1 Depressed patients vs. healthy persons and significant differences in SEEKING, PLAY, FEAR, and SADNESS (no significant differences in CARE and ANGER – therefore not depicted). Data from Montag et al. (2017). The Y-axis depicts the answer format ranging from 1 = totally disagree to 4 = totally agree.

of higher-order continuum models in psychiatry/psychology is very modern and it shows that humans tend more or less to one of the directions on a continuum, with the opposing poles being not depressed or very depressed. Clearly, a psychiatrist needs the label "depression" to provide the patient with the correct treatment, but humans naturally show more or less depression tendencies in either direction on the continuum. The same logic has been already applied to personality in Chapter 2. For an easy to remember summary, the activity of the primary emotional systems underlying depression – SEEKING, (PLAY),[2] SADNESS, and FEAR – is depicted in Figure 3.1.

Another very important insight from Jaak's research concerns the nature of addiction. Addiction comes in many forms

2   Please note that PLAY was also lower in the depressed patient group compared to the healthy controls.

aside from substance-dependent addictions (such as alcohol or nicotine addiction), and the scientific community is focusing more and more on non-substance dependent addictions such as pathological gambling, but also the overuse of Internet, smartphones and related devices.[3] First of all (and this will be a "shocker" to many, as Jaak puts it), the molecules underlying addictive behavior are often the same molecules we know from the neuroscience of love! For example, both consuming a drug as well as being in love can result in elevated opioid levels in the brain (Panksepp et al. 1978). This idea has been supported by many other researchers in the neurosciences, showing a strong overlap of the biochemistry underlying love and addiction. This surprising fact becomes more understandable when we take a closer look at a short history of modern drug use. Here, we refer to a sketch from the excellent book, *Drugs without the Hot Air,* by leading addiction researcher Dr. David Nutt. In the simple Figure 4.7 on page 62 of his book, Dr. Nutt describes how the historical origin of drugs can be traced back to plants developing/producing substances that were originally meant to avert predators (Nutt 2012). Therefore, plants' production of these substances initially presented a protection mechanism to reduce the danger of being consumed. As part of the evolutionary process, animals (including mammals) started to overcome their aversion to these "protective substances" and started to actually like them. Finally, *Homo sapiens* not only learned how to extract the substances from plants, but also managed to synthesize similar substances in the lab to use them either for recreational purposes or self-medication. All cultures we know of use drugs, to some extent, to modify their emotional state of mind. In every case, as we will see in the next paragraph, drugs resonate strongly within the neural circuitries underlying primal emotional systems and modulate our positive and negative emotions.

Returning to our example dealing with love and addiction, Jaak revealed several psychological parallels when contrasting an addict quitting "cold turkey" (in withdrawal by stopping all at once) with a lovesick person (a socially dependent person experiencing a relationship break up and separation distress).

3   See also Chapter 5.

To outline and explain this a bit further, we present the word pairs as described by Jaak in a sketch from his textbook *Affective Neuroscience* (Panksepp 1998), contrasting the drug addict versus the love sick person: The drug addict feels psychic pain while the love-sick person is lonely. The condition of drug addiction often results in anorexic tendencies, while loss of appetite is typical for many lovesick persons. The drug addict often experiences insomnia, while the lovesick person is sleepless. Drug addicts in withdrawal tend to show aggressive behavior, while lovesick persons sometimes demonstrate irritated behavior. Of special importance, the comparison of drug addiction withdrawal with lovesickness also helps us to understand why many lovesick persons try to medicate themselves with alcohol or other drugs, and while individuals with a background of poor relationships (perhaps starting in their families as children) are prime candidates for opioid addiction.

In short, separation distress triggers the SADNESS system, which simply feels awful. In order to stop this awful feeling, humans consume drugs, which initially diminish the emotional pain elicited from the SADNESS system. Unfortunately, the side effects are well known and drug addiction itself very likely causes further and deeper states of depression. Here, major depressive symptoms result when the drug is either not working anymore due to development of tolerance (higher doses are needed to experience the same effect of the drug), or the drug is not accessible anymore and the drug addict experiences a phase of strong withdrawal. Importantly, both *physical pain* and *psychological pain* due to the loss of a personal relationship likely feel very much the same. How do we know that? Well, brain scans reveal that experiencing the loss of a person results in comparable brain activity to when one experiences physical pain. Jaak summarizes: "That is the way evolution works, by using preexisting solutions for crafting new tools for living" (Panksepp and Biven 2012, 323). The preexisting solution for signaling bodily harm was physical pain, a concept reused in the evolutionary development of our brains to signal loss of personal connection resulting in psychological pain (Panksepp 2003).

Aside from depression and drug addiction, Jaak's AN theory also helps to understand other mental disorders such as schizophrenia. Although schizophrenia is a very complex disorder of the human mind, some of the key characteristics for many (but clearly not all) afflicted patients are "positive" symptoms such as auditory hallucinations. Positive symptoms in the context of schizophrenia refer to something that is perceived by a schizophrenic person that was not perceived when the patient was healthy. For example, the patients hear voices talking to them (acoustic hallucinations). It is well known that one of the key neurotransmitter systems involved with schizophrenia is the molecule dopamine. Schizophrenia, among other mental disorders, is characterized by excess levels of dopamine in the SEEKING system. Neuroleptics given as part of the treatment of schizophrenia aim at the down regulation of the SEEKING system via blocking dopaminergic pathways, because the over activity of SEEKING might be the causal factor for the positive symptoms accompanying schizophrenia. The effects of an under activity of the SEEKING system have already been characterized above in the context of depression. Both the states of schizophrenia and depression demonstrate how important it is for our well-being that our primal emotions are in balance! For more stimulating insights about which dysfunction of primary emotions might underlie different forms of mental disorders, please see another paper by Jaak (Panksepp 2006).

From Christian's perspective: as we have seen from the example of the small child getting lost in the supermarket or the break up of the couple, Jaak's AN theory is able to illustrate how we cope emotionally with many everyday situations, which is relevant not only to our understanding of the dysfunctions of the human mind, but also, to a great extent, to how we react to evolutionarily significant situations affecting our personal well-being. Another interesting example illustrating the SADNESS circuitry is homesickness. Many of us stick to a greater (or lesser) degree to our hometown. It often represents the place where we grew up and many have fond childhood memories attached to this place. I was born in Cologne, Germany, on the beautiful Rhine River. It is a village of one million inhabitants, founded by the Romans about 2,000 years ago. Cologne is famous for many things; perhaps most well known are the Cologne Cathedral (also called the "Dom"), the Cologne Carnival and the Cologne beer called

Fig. 3.2 On the left, the famous Cologne panorama is depicted with the Cologne cathedral. On the right, Christian spotted the Cologne cathedral (*Dom*) on a Chinese advertisement for a German language course at the campus of the University of Electronic Science and Technology of China (UESTC) in Chengdu, China and felt a little bit homesick (mild SADNESS activity).

"Kölsch," which is also the name for the local German dialect spoken by natives of Cologne. So, "Kölsch" is the only language you can drink! My job as a researcher comes with lots of worldwide travel opportunities. In addition to my work in China and other countries internationally, I commute in Germany between my hometown of Cologne and my position in Ulm. It is a three-hour ride by high-speed train. I like traveling very much and I adjust to foreign environments quickly. But no matter where I am, thinking of my hometown results in (mild) homesickness, because I am away from a place I am really attached to. Needless to say, it's not only the place, but especially the people who are affiliated with the place that cause the separation distress (and, hence, activity in the SADNESS system). For many people from Cologne, just seeing the cathedral on a picture while far away from home (see Figure 3.2) triggers homesickness via activity of the SADNESS circuitry.

These illustrations on homesickness also fit very well with results from experiments in a closely related lab (led by J.P. Scott) at Bowling Green State University (where Jaak worked for many years before going to Washington State University), which demonstrated that distress vocalizations (DVs) are strongest in young guinea pigs (Pettijohn 1979) as well as young puppies (Pettijohn et al. 1977) when they are alone in a strange place. The crying is reduced but still high when the guinea pigs are alone in their own home. Of note, when mom is there, the place does not play a role anymore. In both the strange place or at home, DVs are nearly nonexistent when mom is there. So, being in a familiar environment (e.g., the area where you have grown up) can reduce SADNESS activity, but what always works best is having your close ones around!

Summary

AN theory effectively explains in simple terms which imbalances of primal emotions underlie a range of mental disorders. In the present chapter, we demonstrated the role of low SEEKING and high FEAR and SADNESS in the state of depression. We also briefly touched on the areas of schizophrenia and addiction and related them to Panksepp's primary emotional systems. Finally, the common feeling of homesickness is explained, again using the example of separation distress. In modern biological psychiatry, researchers aim to understand mental disorders as disorders rooted in the human brain (we focused on primal emotions arising from ancient brain regions in the present chapter). Hence, we are always dealing with organic disorders, even when we are facing the often "bizarre" and tragic world of mental disorders. Seen this way, a patient with back pain has organic issues with his/her back, but someone with depression or schizophrenia has organic issues with his/her brain. Hopefully, this kind of view of mental disorders will be able to reduce much of the stigma still prevailing in our society with respect to people suffering from psychopathologies.

SADNESS

The organ was playing the sad notes of a well-known song in a dialect from Cologne. My hands tightly gripped the handle of the coffin. One of my closest friends had died at the age of thirty from a rare genetically inherited disorder. Together with five of his friends, I was carrying him in the coffin out of the church and towards his grave. As we bore his coffin, images from our shared school days, from many carnival parties, and our last trip to Formentera, a small island near Ibiza, flashed before my eyes, but so too did images from the last horrible months in which he'd suffered so much. I simply felt miserable and could not imagine at this point that he was gone forever.

4

On the Dilemma of Animal Emotions and Eating Animals

Both the United States of America and Germany are pet friendly. In the U.S. alone, household pets include 94.2 million cats and 89.7 million dogs (Statista Research Department 2017). In Germany, we see much lower, but still high numbers: 14.8 million cats and 9.4 million dogs ("Heimtiermarkt Deutschland" 2019). We are pretty sure that if we asked most of the owners of these pets if their animals feel emotions or if they have personalities, the clear answer would be yes! Here, an interesting gap exists between what is accepted as common knowledge in the broad lay population and what science says about this topic. It is pretty astonishing that only a few scientists dare to have an opinion on this delicate topic (although numbers are growing), in particular when one considers that animals share a lot of their emotional makeup with our own. Many scientists may have an opinion on this topic, but clearly it is not that easy to prove with scientific means that animals indeed have emotions.

The topic at hand is very sensitive. If our society comes (and it must come) to the final conclusion that our fellow animals suffer and also experience joy and pain, this would hopefully have tremendous consequences for animal welfare. Are we allowed to conduct experiments on animals? Are we allowed to eat animals? In order to help you to find your own answers to these important questions, we would like to stress two areas of relevant research. First, however, we note the current distressing condition of many animal factory farms, including the depressed state of people working in this industry (yes, the bloody job of slaughtering animals causes psychic pain in many of these workers), as reported in Jonathan Safran Foer's bestselling book, *Eating Animals* (2010).

Foer summarizes in a drastic but necessary way that eating animals might, in the end, also have consequences for our species and our own well-being: "When we eat factory-farmed meat we live, literally, on tortured flesh. Increasingly, that tortured flesh is becoming our own" (143).

The first area we now discuss summarizes several points concerning animal emotions that we've already mentioned in this book. The second area will deal with animal personalities and also offers our opinion on eating animals, backed up by some recent scientific evidence.

With respect to animal emotions, a major reason for the large gap between what is accepted, on the one hand, by broad parts of the population and, on the other, by the scientific community, clearly has to do with the *behaviorist* tradition that burst forth in the psychological discipline in the early twentieth century. In the 1920s and 1930s, psychological scientists such as John Broadus Watson and Burrhus Frederic Skinner denied the importance of studying emotions and relied simply on stimulus–response models. Presenting a rat with a cue (the stimulus) predicting the possibility of receiving a food pellet and recording the behavior (the response) of the rat was sufficient for them to gain insights into mammalian (and human) behavior. Although the field has profited from this approach because it fostered a model of well-controlled experiments and a focus on statistically driven psychological research, it completely denied the affective or cognitive processes of a person/animal.

A shift in this research paradigm – in particular with respect to the study of emotions – was made possible with the development of new methods of studying the human mind. In direct opposition to the behaviorist tradition, direct stimulation of the brain – both electrically and chemically – to directly probe its secrets was among Jaak Panksepp's favorite tools in his animal research. In addition, techniques such as magnetic resonance imaging enable scientists to record brain activity in areas where emotional activity can be triggered in humans (Markett et al.

2018). With brain imaging techniques, correlates of emotions between animals and humans in various situations are made visible.

Summarizing what we know through Jaak's work (and clearly also from many of his fine colleagues), the old layers of our human brains share abundant similarities with animals from our fellow mammalian family (Panksepp 2005). Those brain regions, where ancient emotions arise and influence our everyday life with activity in the SEEKING, CARE, LUST, PLAY, RAGE, SADNESS, or FEAR systems, are quite comparable across mammalian species. Not only is the brain anatomy comparable in many ways, but what happens when these brain circuitries are electrically or chemically stimulated by researchers is also, to some extent, comparable. Naturally, in humans, this research is hard to conduct (due to ethical restraints). Still, we know from patients who undergo brain surgery that their emotions can also be manipulated by external electrical stimulation of ancient brain structures, leading to energetic SEEKING feelings when the medial forebrain bundle is the target of the stimulation (Bewernick et al. 2017; Coenen et al. 2011). The latter knowledge is also already used experimentally to treat treatment-resistant depressed patients.

We argue (along with Jaak Panksepp) that electric stimulation of these brain areas in both mice and men likely not only leads to comparable emotional feelings (at least to some extent), but also to similar action patterns. Such action patterns could be approach with SEEKING and avoidance with FEAR.[1] In short, the abundant evidence from neuroscientific work shows that animal emotions must exist. On an experiential level, those emotions must be rawer in animals, as they are less regulated compared to humans with our well-developed thinking caps. But it is also true that some ambiguities concering the experience of emotions in mammals will never be resolved. As Jaak put in a paper from 2005:

Thus, we may not be able to monitor the specific types of taste qualia a cow experiences when eating high or low qual-

---

1   See also brain imaging evidence for the FEAR circuitry in humans (Mobbs et al. 2007).

ity hay; we may never know whether their experiences are of delightful sweetness or bland starch, or something else quite unimaginable to us. However, with approach and avoidance measures, we can determine that certain experiences are aversive and others pleasant, and that there are many distinct forms of positivity and negativity, with some experiences being more positive or negative than others. (45)

Going one step further, we want to explore the question of whether animals have personalities. As outlined earlier in Chapter 2, individual differences in primary emotional systems could be seen as the evolutionary origins of human personality that shape our personalities into becoming, for example, introverted vs. extraverted. Here we argued that the PLAY system is likely a crucial bottom-up driver of Extraversion and the primary emotion of SEEKING the foundation of the personality trait of Openness to Experience. To make a long story short, if we follow this thought further down the road, it is reasonable to expect that personality traits are not only observable in humans, but are also likely to occur in other mammals, because, as we've already seen, individual differences in animal emotions are likely the evolutionarily oldest parts of personality. And indeed, there is evidence for animal personality. Studies dealing with dogs (Gosling, Kwan, and John 2003) have demonstrated that dogs might share four out of the Big Five personality traits as registered in human psychological research.[2] With the exception of Conscientiousness, research using dogs rated by independent observers who were not previously familiar with the dogs resulted in comparable measures of Extraversion, Openness to Experience, Agreeableness, and Neuroticism. Recent research has shown that Conscientiousness might be the one personality trait out of the Big Five relying most strongly on cognitive areas of the brain (the evolutionary layer more recently added to our brains). Importantly, aside from humans, conscientious behavior has only been reliably observed in our closest evolutionary relative, the chimpanzee, and perhaps in another cortically well-

2 See also work on the general research approach with respect to animal personality (Gosling 2001).

endowed primate, the brown capuchin monkey (Altschul et al. 2017; Morton et al. 2013).

What do we do with these findings? It seems very likely that animals feel emotions, that they have, to some degree, comparable personalities to humans and that, at the bottom of our minds, we share an ancient experiential treasure. Are we then allowed to eat animals, and are we allowed to carry out experiments on them?

Without a doubt, animal research is of importance to humans, and therefore, from our perspective, under strict guidelines, scientists should probably be allowed to conduct experiments with animals. Why? Unfortunately, we simply do not have the ability to understand the deepest secrets in our brains without research using our fellow mammalian sisters and brothers. Without such an understanding, we will not be able to develop new and better treatments for mental disorders, which cause so much pain for patients around the globe (just remember the number of 264 million depressed patients worldwide). By sacrificing the lives of rodents and other mammals in the most extreme form of animal research, the psychic pain of many humans can be alleviated.[3] As the final proofs of this book are being edited, the emergence of the coronavirus and treatments for this pandemic flu illustrate that medical research also relies (even more heavily) on rats and mice to develop the cures that we come to rely on.

This said, the pursuit of knowledge about animal emotions comes with special responsibilities that need to be taken strongly into account when researchers aim at conducting such animal studies. We need to make sure that the animals have as much comfort as possible and, obviously, that they only ever experience the lowest possible amount of pain (if any) for the research question at hand. Clearly, animal research should always include the lowest number of creatures needed to answer the scientific question at hand. Moreover, it should always be determined by an ethical board whether or not the scientific question to be studied is important enough to warrant animal participation. Naturally,

3   It should be noted that invasive research on chimpanzees has been shut down around the world, and the U.S. National Institutes of Health ended support for chimpanzee research in 2015.

it is easier and less problematic to do a study investigating positive emotions such as joy (tickling rats) than eliciting FEAR or
SADNESS in animals.

Luckily, today we have strong ethical restrictions for conducting research, not only on humans, but also on other animals.
Every researcher in this area knows about the burdensome but
necessary paperwork to be done to support such research. Given
the many studies conducted by Jaak on the animal brain, we want
to mention that Jaak Panksepp himself was a strong advocate of
animal welfare. In his book, *Affective Neuroscience,* he describes
his personal view on this important issue: "The debate over the
use of live animals in behavioral and biomedical research cannot
be resolved by logic. [...] The practice of animal research has to be
a trade-off between our desire to generate new and useful knowledge for the betterment of the human condition, and our wish
not to impose stressors on other creatures which we would not
impose on ourselves" (Panksepp 1998, 199). If you are interested
in this area beyond our short discussion, we strongly encourage
you to read the complete passage from the above citation.

From our perspective, because of the sheer number of sacri-
ficed/suffering animals, our eating habits represent a much bigger problem for overall animal welfare than scientifically driven
animal experiments. These numbers illustrate our point: "We eat
over 340 chickens for each animal used in a research facility, and
almost 9,000 chickens for every animal used in research covered
by the Animal Welfare Act. For every animal used in research,
it is estimated that 14 more are killed on our roads" (Speaking
of Research 2020). Don't get us wrong, each animal suffering is
very SAD no matter if there is a scientific purpose or an industrial
animal factory behind the suffering. But economically and eco-
logically speaking, everything counts more in large amounts. It
is well known that the current (and still dramatically growing)
numbers of humans on our planet, together with their wish to
consume more and more meat, represents an unholy coalition.
There is simply not enough "natural" available meat for the
current 7.8 billion inhabitants on this globe (Worldometers.
info 2020). Mass production of animal meat causes numerous
problems in our current world and will do so for generations to
come. Aside from the pain afflicted on those many incarcerated

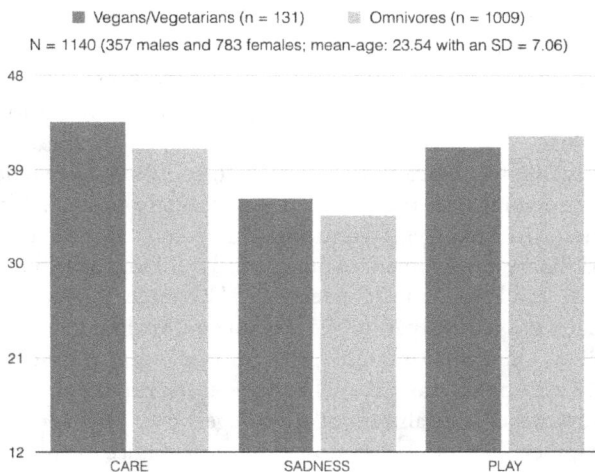

Fig. 4.1 Differences when contrasting vegans/vegetarians and omnivores in the context of primary emotional systems according to AN theory. Note that a score between 12 and 48 could be achieved on each of the depicted scales. Higher scores indicate higher trait CARE, SADNESS, and PLAY.

animals, we also destroy our environment when more and more animal farms are needed to "produce" ever-larger amounts of meat. For example, a not negligible issue is the excrement these incarcerated animals produce, which needs to be disposed of somewhere and is also a source of significant pollution for the soil (just think of the scores of antibiotics mixed into animal food finding their way into the animals' excrement). Moreover, it is well known that the earth's rain forests are further destroyed each year due to clear cutting to create more farmland needed to plant soybeans (a monoculture), which is then used as food for animal mass production. Beyond this, the massive consumption of meat stemming from industrialized animal farms causes problems for humans in terms of developing resistance to antibiotics.

As humans tend to have problems in changing their habits and behaviors, is it time to have stricter guidelines implemented by governments with respect to our diets, such as nudging humans toward less consumption of meat? Just think of the success of the anti-tobacco campaign in many countries. Is it imaginable or feasible to also do this with respect to the consumption of meat from animal factories? Probably not, but we need to think about solutions.

This said, we also can't deny our heritage. *Homo sapiens* have been carnivores over the complete evolutionary process. Many theories exist linking the consumption of cooked meat to the extraordinary development of our cortical thinking cap (Fonseca-Azevedo and Herculano-Houzel 2012). Therefore, consumption of meat was a natural part of the human diet, leading to what we are today. Of further interest, although evidence is still preliminary (Key, Appleby, and Rosell 2006), vegetarians seem to have few advantages (but also no disadvantages) over carnivores due to their diets (with the exception of a better chance of surviving ischemic heart disease). Nevertheless, the saying "We are what we eat" is true to some extent. Further, we have lost our respect for the many lives given by the animals that end up on our plates, because clearly it made a difference when our ancestors chased an animal while hunting compared to the processes observed in factory farms producing meat in unbelievable quantities. Whether or not we decide to abstain completely from eating meat, our world would benefit if human meat consumption were reduced globally.

We close this chapter by comparing personality characteristics of carnivores and omnivores compared to vegetarians and vegans. In a study led by Rayna Sariyska, we asked a large number of participants to fill out the ANPS (Sariyska et al. 2019). When contrasting the different diet groups in light of individual differences in primary emotional systems, we observed higher CARE and SADNESS in vegetarians/vegans compared to omnivores. PLAY scores were lower in those not eating animals (see Figure 4.1). Please also note that, while the differences are statistically significant, they should not be overstressed, due to rather low effect sizes of the differences.

Summary

Mounting evidence strongly points toward the idea that animals (in particular our fellow mammals) share primal emotions with us. Animals may experience these emotions in more raw form, because in the adult human brain, evolutionarily newer brain layers often regulate the energy arising from the ancient circuitries.

It also seems to be the case, at least to some extent, that mammals have personalities comparable with human personalities. Deriving from this, we argue for the importance of at least limiting our meat consumption. This is also needed to protect the environment because "meat production" relies heavily on many scarce resources. Moreover, to foster animal welfare, strict regulations for animal research are mandatory.

CARE

I looked into my daughter's eyes. She was born a few days before and I was rocking her to sleep. Everything about her looked so small and fragile. Such small fingers and such small toes! They looked like little pearls to me. The cute look on her face triggered an unconditional urge in me to CARE for her. Her crying minutes ago caused me psychic pain. If my little girl feels bad, I also feel bad. It's as easy an equation as this.

5

Of Primal Emotional Needs
in a Digital Society

A German kid is sitting in front of his computer and shouts at the screen: "I want to play *Ultimate Tournament!*" This kid is probably in his early teens and produces a guttural cry, which is followed by verbal iterations on really wanting to play this video game. What follows is a disturbing video of a teenager RAGING at the computer and finally destroying the keyboard because the computer is not loading the game (Beatz 2007). This video has been watched nearly two million times on YouTube. Whether this video was staged or not (the protagonist states in a later video that it was actually acted out (Fleischer 2018)), it becomes clear that, for a lot of young children and adolescents, the computer represents a hard to resist temptation, with its many attractive video games and the abundant possibilities of the world wide web. In times of the ubiquitously available smartphone and in addition to the aforementioned video games, online social networks such as Facebook and Instagram or messenger services such as WhatsApp and WeChat are of great interest to teenagers and also growing numbers of older online users. In our own research (Montag et al. 2015), we demonstrated that the average (and directly tracked) smartphone usage of more than 2,400 investigated participants, ranging mostly between 14 and 35 years old, was about 32 minutes daily on WhatsApp. WhatsApp is an application on a smartphone that a person can use to easily exchange messages with an individual or with a group of people. It is even possible to send around pictures or videos via these channels. WhatsApp is so successful that currently over one billion people have already installed it on their smartphones. This means that about every seventh person on this globe has created a WhatsApp account. The app WeChat is comparable to WhatsApp, but actually represents an even more powerful application (you can also pay with it), and dominates the mobile market in China (Montag, Becker, and Gan 2018). Typically, the complete peer group of any given teenager is spending a great deal of time on these digital channels. Importantly, it is nearly impossible for a single young person to quit using such messaging apps, because one would risk being socially rejected from the group with the likely consequence of feeling left out and alone and experiencing intense separation-distress/SADNESS. We will try to revisit and solve this issue when discussing real PLAY behavior in the last section of this chapter.

One of the countries with the highest incidence of digital overusage is South Korea. Here, about 5% of the population (two million inhabitants), has been reported to be "hooked on" the online world (Hartvig 2010). One reason for this unbelievably high number is that one of the main industries providing jobs to people in South Korea is the computer industry. In this case, the same industry that provides jobs and a means of making a living also fosters addictive tendencies. In order to address the problem, several years ago, the government of South Korea launched an official initiative to fight Internet addiction. As a result, psychological counseling has been provided for thousands of patients in this Asian country. Although problems in other countries are still comparably low, the rest of the industrialized world is catching up fast in terms of overusing digital technologies. According to representative numbers (Rumpf et al. 2011), one percent of the German population was Internet addicted with numbers rising, and in 2014, the figure was already at two percent (Müller et al. 2014). Just take a look at what people are doing every day on public transportation! Everyone stares at a small device, their attention completely absorbed. To some extent, all digital societies are facing problems due to overusage of smartphones and the Internet.[1]

1 At the beginning of this chapter we already noted that Internet

Beyond these numbers, the press has covered many other disturbing stories in the last years that go beyond what we've already mentioned in this chapter. There was an unbelievable and very SAD story about parents letting their baby starve because they were focused instead on feeding a cyber baby (Tran 2010). In another story, a young man shot and killed his mother and wounded his father because they took away his video game (Martinez 2009). Further fatalities have been reported in the context of Internet addiction due to cardiopulmonary arrest after binge video gaming for several days without stopping (Hunt and Ng 2015). In Christian's hometown of Cologne, Germany, special traffic lights are being tested for pedestrians who stare at their smartphones instead of paying attention to traffic. In New Jersey, in the U.S., there is a proposal to ban texting on smartphones while walking (Billig 2016).

Although these cases resonate in the neural circuitry underlying our ancient negative emotions, fortunately, in their extreme form, they are infrequent, and we do not want to overpathologize everyday life habits that often provide us with joy. Needless to say, technologies are often very helpful in enabling communication across large distances. Christian could not live without Skype or other communication platforms when he's doing his research in China and longing to see his wife, Susanne, and daughter, Hannah.

Nevertheless, the introduction of digital technologies brings both opportunities *and* risks/problems. As the positive aspects of digital technologies are fairly obvious (again, just think of the great global communication possibilities or the fact that Ken and Christian could write this book together), in the present chapter we focus on the darker sides of technology usage. The dramatic changes in society due to the digital revolution and its impact on personal communications and on business has also impacted the scientific community, where a growing number of researchers around the globe are trying to understand if problematic Internet

addiction represents no official diagnosis. In general, researchers abstain from using the term "Internet addiction," but instead speak of "problematic Internet use" or "Internet Use Disorder." In this chapter, we use the term "Internet addiction" only for reasons of simplicity.

use is, indeed, best characterized as an addiction. Notably, there is clear evidence that at least some of the same neural circuitries of the brain are involved in "Internet addiction" that are seen with other forms of substance (or non-substance) addictions such as alcohol addiction or pathological gambling.[2] Moreover, in June 2018, the World Health Organization included Gaming Disorder in ICD-11. The International Classification of Disease (ICD, now in version 11) is a manual in which psychiatric disorders are described in detail. With the inclusion of Gaming Disorder in ICD-11, a specific form of Internet addiction, perhaps better called Internet Use Disorder, has been accepted and designated as an official disease/brain disorder.[3]

Until the general debate on the nature of Internet addiction is ultimately settled (and it takes time to do good science), we urgently need to answer some pressing questions. What status should technology have in our lives in the future? When and how should we use it? At what age should children be allowed to have first contact with a smartphone? The list of such questions is already very long (and gets longer by the day). Although empirical evidence to answer these questions is rare, we might not have much time to answer them, because: i) the technological progress in our digital society is happening in ever-faster cycles and; ii) if there are negative consequences to be faced due to digital overuse, it might be too late for several generations already growing up with and using these technologies every day. In the following section, we would like to attempt to find some answers to these pressing questions by taking into account some insights from AN theory.

Before continuing, we wish to reiterate that we do not want to be one-sided about the manifold aspects of the Internet. Without a doubt, the Internet is a fantastic technology connecting people around the world. And in fact, many of our scientific papers would have not been written without the ability to communicate with other researchers via email. This was particularly true for Christian's cooperation with Jaak. Just like

2   But there are also differences; see a recent review by Montag and Becker (2019).
3   Note that this diagnosis was ratified in May 2019.

millions of people every day, we enjoy the Internet and stimulate our SEEKING systems by searching for infotainment or snooping through the latest research articles being published ever more frequently in open access journals. These scientific articles can even be downloaded at no cost to interested readers. However, all these positive aspects of the Internet do not mean that we should close our eyes to the potentially harmful consequences of digital overusage. Here, we would like to highlight some thoughts that might lead some of our readers to reconsider their own digital consumption.

Okay, what's going wrong in our digital societies? Before becoming too academic, we briefly note that we will not be very precise in the following, because Internet addiction is not necessarily exactly the same as smartphone addiction or other forms of digital overusage. Indeed, research from other groups in addition to our own demonstrates that some overlap between these digital addictions exists, but naturally, there is also room for differences. For instance, many people might think of desktop computers and video games when confronted with the term "Internet addiction," and not of the Internet per se when thinking about their Internet connected smartphones. Perhaps Internet addiction is also simply an umbrella term for mobile and non-mobile forms of Internet addiction (Montag et al. 2020); time will tell. Notably, if the Gaming Disorder diagnosis in ICD-11 one day functions as a blueprint for other forms of Internet addiction, it might be of interest to know that all four of the following items in the recently published Gaming Disorder Test (Pontes et al. 2019, see overleaf) need to be positively answered in order to indicate an addiction to video games.

Beyond these recent developments and academic debates, it is fairly obvious that one of the leading problems of digital addictive tendencies is the smartphone and its manifold applications (Montag et al. 2020; Sha et al. 2019). It may be particular noteworthy that Steve Jobs, who successfully ushered in the smartphone hype with the iPhone in 2007, did not allow his own children to use an iPad and was very strict with his children with respect to the use of digital devices in general (Bolton 2016). This is interesting, because Steve Jobs was obviously a very smart man (some claimed he was a genius). Given that he is responsible

Gaming Disorder Test

Instructions: The questions below are about your gaming activity during the past year (i.e., last 12 months). Here, gaming activity means any gaming-related activity that has been played either from a computer/laptop or from a gaming console or any other kind of device (e.g., mobile phone, tablet, etc.) both online and/or offline.

Notably, the following items are presented in past tense, as you are asked to describe your gaming activity during the last twelve months. Nevertheless, when answering the items, please keep in mind that we explicitly refer to a time window *starting twelve months ago up until today.*

1. I have had difficulty controlling my gaming activity.
2. I have given increasing priority to gaming over other life interests and daily activities.
3. I have continued gaming despite the occurrence of negative consequences.
4. I have experienced significant problems in life (e.g., personal, family, social, education, occupational) due to the severity of my gaming behavior.

for the fact that a large number of digital gadgets can be found in everyone's pocket nowadays, these strict parenting practices might come as a surprise. Maybe he just foresaw some of the problems we are discussing in this chapter – in particular for the young, vulnerable brains of children.

Why is the smartphone so "addictive"? We are convinced that one reason many people are hooked on their smartphones is due to slot machine strategies at work in several applications on these small devices.[4] In psychology, we refer to the reinforcement strategy operating on smartphones as *intermittent reward,* meaning not being able to predict *when* you will receive the next reward (but knowing that it *will* come). In other words, when we are checking our phones, we are not getting rewarded every single time. The kinds of small rewards we are referring to could be a nice message from a loved one, a funny message on Facebook, and, for scientists, a message about an accepted research paper coming in via email. This simple operant learning mechanism results in steady responding, gluing millions of people to their phones, which, in Germany, gave rise to the slang word *smombies* – smartphone zombies. In fact, in 2015, this was acknowledged as an official slang word used by teenagers. As mentioned above, in Christian's hometown we even have traffic lights anchored in the pavement so that smombies don't get run over by the train when crossing the street (Montag 2018)!

What is also troubling to see is that attendees of concerts choose to record the complete music performance on their smartphones instead of enjoying the concert. This costs a lot of cognitive focus (holding the smartphone stable without shaking the device in the dark). Following from this, the concert attendee is not emotionally involved and produces a bad video in the dark that will probably never be watched anyway. In short, the old Roman saying *carpe diem* (retranslated for our times as "seize the day") is not valued anymore, as we regularly distract ourselves from the actually occurring event (Montag and Walla 2016). For example: romantic couples who prefer their smartphones instead

4 Of relevance, persons are not addicted to the smartphone, but to applications on the phone. Alcoholics are also not addicted to a bottle, but to the content of the bottle (Panova and Carbonell 2018).

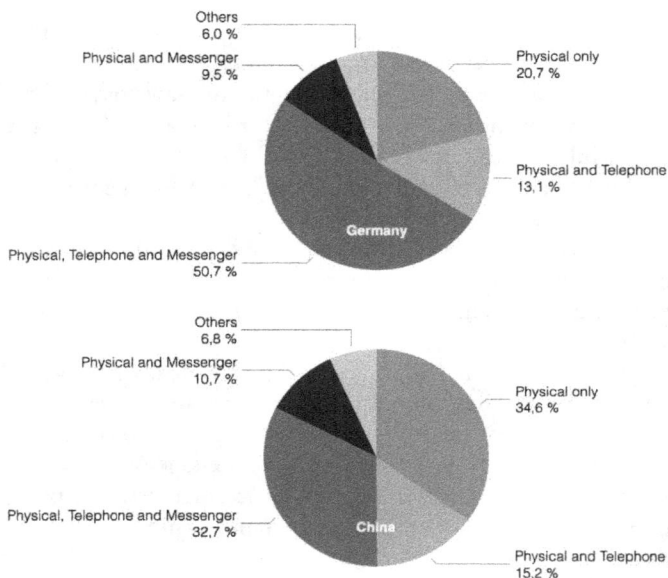

Fig. 5.1 603 German participants (170 males and 433 females; $M_{age} = 23.10$, $SD_{age} = 8.13$); 871 Chinese participants (656 male and 215 female; $M_{age} = 21.43$, $SD_{age} = 2.27$) were asked what kind of social support they would prefer when feeling SAD.

of talking to each other, even when having a candlelight dinner. Then there is the young girl Christian observed some years ago going through the zoo in Singapore – sadly, she was more interested in her smartphone than in the wildlife activity around her. Christian previously covered this story in his book *Homo Digitalis,* published in German (Montag 2018).

Returning to our questions: What status should technology have in our lives in the future? When and how should we use these technologies? At what age should children be allowed to have first contact with a smartphone? The first two questions have been partly answered by the illustration above (Figure 5.1), and the answers to these questions fit well with our basic needs arising from our ancestral animal emotions: In order to feel good, most well-adjusted adults need direct "face to face"/"human to human" interaction. In particular when feeling SAD, what do you want most? A real hug by a loving, supportive person or an encouraging smiley face via WhatsApp? The answer seems to be fairly clear and is also supported by data from Christian's German and Chinese labs, where, in general, participants were happy with different kinds of support, but clearly chose options including physical support most often (in both Germany and China about 94%!). In short, this shows that we are mammalian beings longing for social support when feeling sad and are happy with different kinds of support. Nevertheless, the physical support still seems to be of highest importance, even in a digital age.

As Jaak Panksepp pointed out in the PANIC/SADNESS/ Loneliness chapter in his book *Affective Neuroscience* (we have mostly referred to it in this book as the SADNESS system), one mechanism to down regulate the SADNESS circuitry of our human brain is via CAREing behavior from close friends and family. Compared to virtual support, a real hug ultimately triggers more production of powerful brain chemicals such as oxytocin and opioids, soothing our emotional pain arising from the activity of the SADNESS brain circuitry.

Let's move to another important topic. Activity of the CARE circuitry might be crucial for explaining empathic abilities in humans. Here, we understand that people are able to put themselves into the shoes of others and, more importantly, also to emotionally feel what another person feels. We wonder what will happen to generations who are used to staring at smartphones instead of nurturing their inborn abilities to read emotions from faces and understand the states of mind of other people they are interacting with. Younger generations from today (also called "digital natives") are not to be blamed. They have not experienced times without digital technologies. Unfortunately, the digital immigrants (here we mean the parental generation of our current children), are often not the role models they should be. How many parents are staring at their own digital devices instead of interacting with their children? On the playground, we often see parents who find it more interesting to fiddle around with their technological devices than to play or interact with their kids. When coming home (tired from work), many parents give their children a tablet to "buy" themselves some silence, although the children are actually longing for attention from the caregiver. This is all lost time for real face-to-face interaction between parents and their children, perhaps with unforeseen consequences for the empathic abilities of their young ones (Lachmann et al. 2018a; Melchers et al. 2015).

We would like to close this chapter with a word on when children should have their first contact with a smartphone or tablet. Naturally, it is hard to answer this question without sound empirical studies. Nevertheless, we know from abundant psychological and neuroscientific studies that regular PLAY activity is key to well-being in children. What is not meant here is PLAY activity on smartphones or a computer game on a console. Instead, mammalian spontaneous rough-and-tumble PLAY requiring no learning might be the most important form of PLAY, fostering social competencies and motor skills of young children. Rough-and-tumble PLAY has been called "the real nasty good stuff for the brain" by Jaak in a video available on YouTube (Panksepp 2010a), pointing towards the fact that this very bodily form of PLAY (roughhousing PLAY) happens spontaneously between play partners without the need to include toys and without guidance from parents (except perhaps to help when someone gets hurt). Children need nothing but themselves to have a good PLAYtime. Bad news for all the fancy toy developers! What has already been shown is a robust link between ADHD and Internet addiction (Sariyska et al. 2015) and ADHD and negative emotionality (Wernicke et al. 2019). Moreover, we observed in our own recent work in young adults (Montag et al. 2016), inverse associations between self-reported PLAY tendencies and the preference for online social interaction (over real life social interaction). Together with studies showing that high Internet addiction tendencies go along with lower empathic traits, we wonder if (real) PLAY deprivation in the form of prolonged screen time might result in tendencies towards ADHD and putatively lower empathic abilities in children as they grow up. Unfortunately, we are all too aware of the fact that we currently have no direct evidence for causal links for the ideas stated here (this theoretical causation is presented in Figure 5.2).

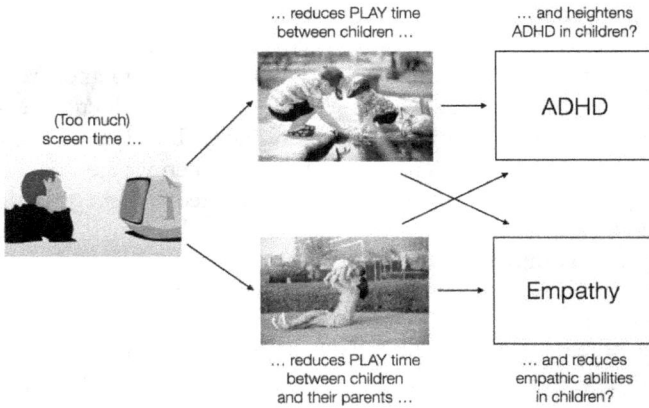

Fig. 5.2 Potential consequences of PLAY deprivation in childhood due to rising screen time.

Nevertheless, given the possibility that we are right, it will not do any harm to send children out with their friends to engage in real rough-and-tumble PLAY with its well-known and proven positive effects. The best side effect of all this will be that, if your child and their friends are all having a good time PLAYing outside, the smartphone will become comparably boring and will be left behind, along with their other digital gadgets. Hence, screen time will naturally decrease. This said, we are not arguing for abstaining in general from digital technologies. For instance, large-scale studies suggest that moderate use in adolescence (after childhood) "is not intrinsically harmful" (Przybylski and Weinstein 2017, 204). As the ancient Greek philosophers have noted – it is important to find the golden mean between too little and too much in nearly all aspects of human life.

Finally, we would also like to focus on the impact of digital technologies on well-being in our work lives. One key concept of well-being has been put forward by psychologist Mihaly Csikszentmihalyi with the so-called *flow* concept (Csikszentmihalyi 2008). Flow describes a state of mind in which we are highly concentrated and forget about time and space, while working in a kind of psychic "rush." One prerequisite for this highly intensive flow experience is a match between our own cognitive ability and the difficulty of the task at hand. We'll return to the flow concept in Chapter 7 when we discuss well-being in the context of our animal emotions. But here we want to stress that flow does not occur at work when we are flooded by distractions such as emails or interrupted by smartphone messages. Ironically, flow often happens in videogames or other digital environments, but the digital influx on our computer and into our lives can also be a stressful experience. Indeed, it has been demonstrated that checking email at planned stable times (instead of checking email always and everywhere) reduces stress (Kushlev and Dunn 2015). Again, see Christian's book *Homo Digitalis* for further ideas on how to better handle the everyday digital influx (Montag 2018).

Another stressful experience is a computer breakdown – in particular in situations in which we rely on technology in order to book a last minute flight or write an important email to a collaborator. In sum, *techno-stress* can result in frustration and then also activate the RAGE circuitry as outlined with our first introductory example of the boy wanting to play his video game (SEEKING). Needless to say, the online world can trigger activity in all of our animal emotions (we have not talked about pornography, substance abuse, and LUST or FEAR triggered by seeing gruesome videos). The most lasting negative impact of digital societies on our well-being might be caused by the mere long hours we spend with digital machines instead of directly CAREing for and about each other. This might also explain negative associations between social media addiction and well-being (Clark, Algoe, and Green 2017; Duradoni, Innocenti, and Guazzini 2020). We end this chapter with a line delivered by Hank Moody, the character played by *X-Files* star David Duchovny. Maybe he was onto something when he said, in episode 4 of season 5 ("Californication"), that he would like to go back to the year 1994 without all the Twitter & Co. stuff.

Summary

Although Internet addiction is not an official diagnosis yet (with the exception of the specific area of Gaming Disorder), this does not mean that we are not facing problems due to digital overuse in many societies around the globe. Changes due to technological (over) use are omnipresent. In the present chapter, we argue that it is of utmost importance for children to act out their inborn PLAYful tendencies in classic ways to develop into psychologically healthy adolescents. Moreover, it is important that children are taken CARE of, whereas parents often make it easy for themselves by putting their children in front of a screen instead of directly interacting with their kids. Finally, also for adults, digital overuse goes along with negative emotionality impacting our SADNESS, FEAR, and ANGER systems.

FEAR

My wife and I were driving a rented Volkswagen Tiguan on a narrow path near Lamar Valley in Yellowstone National Park. Off the beaten track, our car was climbing slowly towards the peak of the mountain. It was a beautiful late summer day and the sun was painting warm colors on the fantastic scenery. I decided to reduce our driving speed to ten miles per hour, because the path was getting narrower and narrower, with a dramatic-looking slope to the right side of the car. Driving around the corner of a sharp left curve, my heart jumped, as a giant buffalo was standing in front of the car. I had no option other than to stop the car and turn off the engine. I froze and waited. The buffalo slowly walked along the left side of the car (with only a very small space left to pass by) and stopped, his left eye staring into mine. This massive buffalo could easily have kicked the car into the abyss on the right side. I was sweating, my heart raced and terror came over me. I was not capable of doing anything at all; I felt paralyzed (a real life example of FEAR-induced "freezing"). After seconds, minutes, or hours – I can't remember – the buffalo slowly started to move on and finally out of sight, as I watched it in the rearview mirror. It took a while until I was myself again. I could read in my wife's eyes that she was emotionally overwhelmed by this encounter as well.

6

The Effects of Music on Our Emotional Brain

"… I acquired a strong taste for music, and used very often to time my walks so as to hear on week days the anthem in King's College Chapel. This gave me intense pleasure, so that my backbone would sometimes shiver."
— Charles Darwin (1958, 61)

After Christmas with the families, my wife and I (CM) were looking forward to some time alone as a couple, getting away from our hometown of Cologne to enjoy some sightseeing in the wonderful city of London (this was before our daughter, Hannah, was born). Moreover, we were keen to attend a concert in one of London's many concert venues. As we were going to attend a classical music concert, my wife, Susanne, and I dressed up a little. On the evening of December 27, 2016, Susanne and I were sitting in London's Barbican Hall to see Katherine Jenkins's Christmas tour (although two days late). I am a big music fan and played guitar myself for a long time in a folk rock/indie band. As a musician and a music lover, I always love it when the lights go down in the concert hall and you feel the emotional energy of the crowd anticipating the show (SEEKING!).

On this evening, the concert hall finally was getting dark and the orchestra started to play Strauss's *Die Fledermaus* followed by Beethoven's *Ode an die Freude* (*Ode to Joy*). If you are not familiar with Katherine Jenkins's music, she is known for performing crossover tunes somewhere between opera, musical, and pop accompanied by a big orchestra. Jenkins is a Welsh mezzosoprano with a stunning voice, and even Her Majesty is known to be a big fan. The concert was a treat, and the crowd was clearly enjoying the performance. There was even a standing ovation at the end of the concert.

Before coming back to Jenkins's (live) performance, we would like to ask: What makes an artist's performance truly unique? In search of a scientific answer, one must consider the ability of an artist to elicit strong emotions in the listener. To outline this a bit more, let me share with you my own experience when I was attending the aforementioned concert. I remember that Mrs. Jenkins performed a Christian hymn called "How Great Thou Art" in the first half of the concert set. This song was originally based both on a Swedish tune and a poem by Carl Gustav Boberg. George Beverly Shea, the soloist for the Billy Graham Crusade for many years, popularized the hymn in the U.S. It has quite a melancholic touch with the song tapering towards a climax at the end. With every passing minute of the song, the musicians of the orchestra played more intensely, getting louder, while Jenkins was singing in the highest regions of her vocal range. While the music was flying through the air, I felt a chill going down my spine. I remember the goose bumps on my skin.

Many readers will be familiar with such an experience (see also Charles Darwin!), although we all differ in terms of how often and how strong these chills occur when we are enjoying music: Some people are simply more prone to experience strong bodily (emotional) reactions to music than others. I myself quite often experience such bodily arousal when confronted with music. We will shed some light on this phenomenon when we turn to aspects of individual differences in "chill experiences" a bit later in this chapter. Moreover, we will revisit some findings from Jaak Panksepp's lab that shed light on the question of which kind of music likely elicits chills.

Before summarizing several highlights of research from our own and other groups, we would like to broadly outline the importance and abundance of music in human life. Perhaps one of the most important reasons why people all around the globe love music is its tremendous effect on the areas of the human brain where our animal emotions are rooted. Specifically, music strongly resonates in our oldest emotional brain circuits and has the ability to induce mood changes. Several fMRI (functional magnetic resonance imaging) experiments have revealed robust activity of parts of the SEEKING system when humans were listening to their favorite music (for those who know more about brain anatomy, it is the ventral striatum – also called the nucleus accumbens – we are referring to). In such an experimental set up, humans are "put into a scanner," where their brain activity can be recorded while acoustic and/or visual stimuli are presented via earphones and/or a screen. The activity of the SEEKING system while listening to our favorite tunes confirms that such musical experiences can be clearly characterized as (very) pleasant. Moreover, as SEEKING activity goes along with feelings of enthusiasm and feelings of strength, music also has the power to energize us. That explains why a lot of professional athletes listen to music while they are training.

That said, music could be used to induce mood changes, but not only in the pleasant direction. Some people use music to enhance their already existing emotional state, such as playing a sad song when already feeling sad. Others use it to counteract their current emotional states, such as playing happy music to counteract one's own negative mood. Studies have explored, from a personality psychologist's point of view, what kinds of music different personality types prefer and how they use it in everyday life (Chamorro-Premuzic, Fagan, and Furnham 2010; Chamorro-Premuzic and Furnham 2007). Among others, it was observed that neurotic, introverted, and less conscientious people used music more frequently for emotional regulation. Given the well-studied effects of music on our moods, music can clearly also be used in a therapeutic way, something which we also cover in this chapter.

We argue that, without the lasting impact of music on our emotional brains, music would not be a multi-billion dollar industry generating 19.1 billion USD worldwide in 2018 (Balda 2020). The high economic value of music mirrors the omnipresence of music in our lives. No matter if we go to a warehouse or to a business event, music is likely present in the background. Commercially, most companies believe that playing the right kind of music will encourage customers to spend more money.

Indeed, there is some scientific evidence for this idea. We've found a paper showing that classical music could stimulate customers to spend more money on expensive wines, thereby showing that music could indeed have an effect on the money leaving your pocket in a shopping mall (Areni and Kim 1993). The mood-changing capacities of music are also well known in Hollywood. Filmmakers use music to enhance the viewer's emotions when watching a movie. Just imagine Hitchcock's famous shower scene in *Psycho* without the rising and unnerving sound of the screeching violins! It simply would not be the same movie. One interesting study observed that the style of music shapes how viewers see a character in a movie. The researchers noted that "thriller music significantly lowered likability and certainty about characters' thoughts" (Hoeckner et al. 2011, 146) when compared to melodramatic music. Such studies are only the beginning and we have just begun to answer how music is able to have such an impact on our moods. Beyond the SEEKING system, other primal emotions are also relevant to understanding why music can crawl under our skin. Let's explore this further.

A study by Panksepp and Bernatzky (2002) demonstrated that listening to either happy or sad music had a profound influence on the mood of the participants. This study, among others, demonstrated that listening to a sad song enhanced sadness, and listening to a happy song enhanced happiness. Further, these effects are strong enough to be statistically significant, but only hold for a short time after the song has ended. This is similar to the short-term effects of pleasant music on increased activity of the nucleus accumbens/ventral striatum and also parallel to the transient effects of electrical brain stimulation of the nucleus accumbens located in the ventral striatum in chronically depressed patients. This means that boosting your mood in a positive way is best achieved by listening to lots of happy music. But, if you stop listening, your mood might change back to the mood level present before listening to the music.

We revisited this work in Christian's lab in Ulm, in the southern part of Germany. The city of Ulm is part of the region called Swabia, a German region known for the food Spätzle and for the penny-pinching tendencies of the local Swabians (don't believe every cliché). The small town of Ulm is famous for having the tallest cathedral in the world,[1] called Ulm Minster (161.5 meters!), and also for the Lion-man (*Löwenmensch*). The Lion-man is a figurine carved from woolly mammoth ivory that was found in Hohlenstein-Stadl (near Ulm). It is the oldest known artifact showing human creativity, dating back 35,000–40,000 years. (By the way, SEEKING activity might be an important driver of creativity (Reuter et al. 2005).[2]) If you ever happen to be in Ulm, it's worth a trip to the museum.

The as yet unpublished and ongoing music research my students and I (CM) carried out was an experiment with eighty people at Ulm University who were listening to different kinds

1 Christian, as a native of Cologne, reluctantly had to accept that Ulm Minster is indeed four meters higher than Cologne cathedral (157 m).

2 A side node on creativity: In Essen's Colosseum I (Christian) had the chance to experience a night with Nick Cave. It was "an evening in conversation with ...", so the audience had the chance to ask him all kinds of questions. I am myself very much interested in creativity, because my job as a scientist requires a good deal of it. In the TV series "Halt and Catch Fire," about the early days of Silicon Valley, the protagonist Joe MacMillan (played by Lee Pace) asks himself at a certain time in the series how much next is still in him? In other words, how often can we reinvent ourselves? This question in this excellent TV show is very much in line with what I more and more ask myself, because I also reinvented myself several times, from a bank accountant to musician to psychologist. Even my research focus has been changing drastically over the years. In sum, this costs energy and at times can become tiring.

After introducing myself, I asked Nick if he also experienced something similar in the past and, if so, what does he do to combat it? He was kind enough to offer an elaborate answer, fully acknowledging that he does not know if creativity in a person is endless, that is, if there is enough creative energy to create something new over and over again. But, in order to avoid repeating himself, he usually finishes a book or the recording process of a new album and then tries to get as far away from the end result as possible. He said that creativity starts to flourish again when he goes into different waters. These waters should be a place where he is not safe, but where he is even facing a bit of discomfort and where risk of failure hangs in the room. This is basically what is happening all the time in science if you engage in interdisciplinary research in which people work together not knowing too much about the collaborating partner's field of research. Thanks, Nick. I agree.

of music via earphones. Immediately before and three times after listening to the songs, the participants were asked to rate their current mood. This was done to assess *if* and *how long* the effects of music would last on the participants' moods. One of the presented songs was a cover version of Sarah MacLachlan's "Angels," performed by the aforementioned Katherine Jenkins. The song was chosen for a reason. First of all, it has quite a melancholic character, which might be particularly able to trigger strong emotions in many listeners.

In the earlier research discussed above, Jaak Panksepp and Günther Bernatzky provided empirical support that it is the high-pitched vocals of a singer that are able to elicit chills, which suggested that the "chill experience," indeed, might be causally linked to separation-calls (crying), triggering (mild) activity in the SADNESS circuitry of the listener's emotional animal brain. They played the song "For Crying Out Loud" by Meat Loaf to the participants of the study. As Marvin Lee Aday, the lead singer of Meat Loaf, is crying out his psychic pain somewhere in the middle of this song, the pain of Mr. Aday can resonate in our own SADNESS circuitry, too. This is reflected by the highest number of chill reports in the middle part of this song. Interestingly, when Panksepp and Bernatzky filtered out the high frequency harmonics of Mr. Aday's "separation-distress cry," the participants' reported chills went down to nearly zero. Here, we see that chills might especially arise from listening to sad music in which the singer of the song mimics human crying. In the meantime, other research has been published dealing with the question of which musical elements might result in higher chill frequencies. In a work by Bannister (2020) with persons listening to the song "Glósóli" by Icelandic post-rock band Sigur Rós, he observed that when this song was played louder, chill experiences increased. So here we have another interesting characteristic of music impacting chill frequencies when listening to it. But what about individual differences in experiencing chills?[3]

3   Shortly before finishing this book, an interesting work was published presenting different categories of chills: warm, cold, and moving chills. Warm chills could reflect more joyful chills, whereas cold chills could be more related to negative affect. Moving chills are "accompanied

Mood Changes due to one's Favorite Song

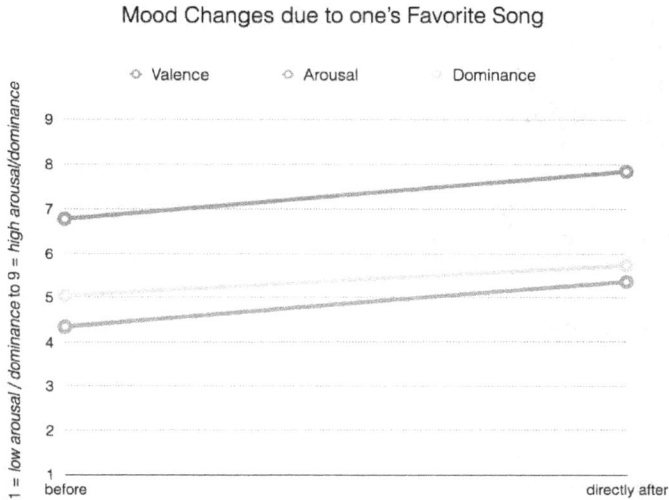

Fig. 6.1 Listening to your favorite song increases happiness (valence), energizes (arousal), and elevates the dominance (feeling of power or control).

Specifically, we know that people who report high empathy seem to more easily experience the SADNESS of others; hence they tend to more strongly feel the singer's emotion. What we are stating here is that emotions carry over from the singer to the listener. In new work from my former student, Mareike Sittler, we were able to show that higher self-reported empathy scores were indeed associated with stronger reported arousal

by bodily activity such as tears and a lump in the throat, and were characterized mainly by feelings of tenderness, affection, intensity, and being moved" (Bannister 2019, 16). The latter category might intensify the warm or cold chills and might be particularly strong in persons with higher empathy. The reader can make up his/her own mind with respect to what category their own experienced chills belong. With respect to some of the bittersweet aspects of some chill experiences - as often experienced when listening to music - we are also not too sure. Much research to do in the future!

(bodily reactions) when listening to positive and negative tunes (Sittler, Cooper, and Montag 2019). In line with Panksepp and Bernatzky's work, music also successfully changed the mood of the participants in our unpublished experiment mentioned earlier and now being explained in greater detail. The main findings of this experiment are also depicted in Figures 6.1 and 6.2.

Before listening to the song "Angel" (see Figure 6.2), all participants were asked to listen to their favorite music, which they had been told to bring along. All participants rated four relevant primal emotions before listening to "Angel," as well as three times after the song was played. With respect to the favorite song condition, we asked for changes in arousal, dominance (how strong do I feel?; how much control do I have?), and how negative/positive do I feel? The results can be seen in Figure 6.1. As one can easily see, listening to one's own favorite tune goes along with elevations in mood, arousal and dominance/power. Hence, due to listening to the favorite song, the participants reported feeling better and stronger. One note: some of the readers of this book might be scientists and will notice that a control group is missing in this experiment. A control group is an important part of experiments allowing the researcher to compare an experimental condition such as listening to one's favorite music with... Yes, what? Indeed, this is the problem here. What would be a good control condition? Listening to one's least-favorite song? No music? Listening to nothing? Well, even silence has been called music by avant-garde artist John Cage, as evidenced in his composition *4'33"*, which he performed live on August 29, 1952, indicating the beginning and ending of the piece just by lifting and closing the lid of his piano. This dilemma shows the problem in choosing the right kind of contrast or control condition in our experimental design. In earlier fMRI work (and needing to find a contrast for one's own favorite music), we asked participants to bring along not only their favorite tune, but also music they really disliked – the latter task was not easy for many to accomplish!

The "Favorite Song" experiment (Figure 6.1) did not measure how long the effects of music would last. Moreover, this experiment does not demonstrate how people react to genuinely sad music (because participants brought along their favorite song,

Mood Changes due to Katherine Jenkins' „Angel"

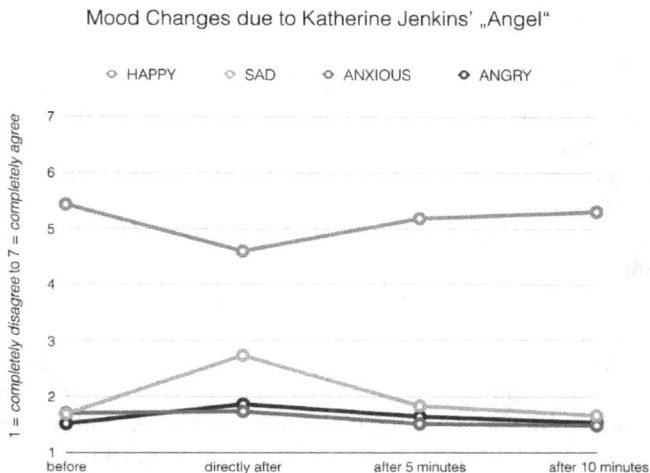

Fig. 6.2 Listening to a sad song reduces feeling happy and elevates feeling sad (although, over all, happiness prevails).

which could be either happy or sad). Along with what has already been introduced from the results of Panksepp and Bernatzky's studies, one would expect strong mood-changing effects of music when participants are confronted with sad music. Here, we refer to the second part of our experiment, in which participants listened to the aforementioned song, "Angel." After listening to this song, participants rated this song as either sad or happy (and, as a group, came to the conclusion that this is a sad song). Moreover, all participants did further mood ratings. This time, these mood ratings happened in the context of specific primary emotional systems. As one can see in Figure 6.2,[4] participants rated their moods to be more sad and less joyful immediately after having listened to this song. It was also clear that such

4 For reasons of completeness, we want to mention that in the experiment participants also listened to a happier song, "Kokomo" by the Beach Boys. The results from this part of the experiment have been less conclusive (as the song was not perceived as happy as we thought). It is therefore not depicted in Figure 6.2.

mood-changing effects do not last long. Five minutes after the song, the mood switched back to the original values, that is, to the mood levels before listening to the song. Moreover, it should be mentioned that these general effects observed across the n = 80 participants (24 males, 56 females; M_{age} = 24.23, SD_{age} = 5.49; one person excluded in Figure 6.1), do vary by individual. For some participants, these feelings are reversed. The sad song is associated with a pleasant feeling. More typically, however, the sad song is clearly experienced as sad.[5]

David Huron mentioned in a paper that the neuropeptide prolactin might explain these reversed effects (Huron 2011). Prolactin is an important hormone in the human body primarily associated with milk secretion in nursing mothers, but it is also known to enhance CAREing behavior in both males and females (as with the neuropeptide oxytocin; see Table 1.1). Huron put forward the idea that humans with high levels of prolactin might experience the sad music as something pleasant, whereas those with low prolactin levels experience the sad music as unpleasant. This idea clearly needs to be tested, as one might also expect that people with high prolactin levels score higher on empathy (more CAREing behavior) and might suffer more from listening to sad music (or rate it to be more unpleasant). While this question requires more research,[6] some additional evidence for the role of prolactin in music perception comes from Christian's lab, showing that a genetic variation on the gene coding for the hormone prolactin is associated with the strength of arousal people experience after being confronted with happy or sad tunes (Sittler, Cooper, and Montag 2019). Hence, we must also take into account the genetic dispositions linked to prolactin neurotransmission when attempting to explain why some people respond strongly to music while others don't care at all.

---

5   We want to mention additional work linking SADNESS to nostalgia, another psychological construct important to the understanding of the effects of sad music on the human brain (Barrett et al. 2010; Barrett and Janata 2016).

6   Shortly before publishing the book a work by Ladinig et al. (2019) was published indicating that Huron's idea lacks empirical support.

Naturally, the molecular underpinnings of the reactions of our minds and bodies to emotional sounds is still poorly understood, and many other molecules, such as oxytocin and norepinephrine, are clearly relevant modulators of the musical experience. A role for these molecules was explored by Larry Normansell (one of Panksepp's Ph.D. students) in his 1988 dissertation, and by Panksepp and Bernantzky, when they played Beethoven and Mozart to little chicks and measured the hormonal changes in their brains. Also noteworthy are recent reports from Bruno Laeng and his students from the University of Oslo working together with Jaak Panksepp, where "chill experiences" could be linked to larger pupil sizes. So, if we pay close attention to the eyes of our fellow music-listening friends, we will see, aside from goosebumps and other bodily changes, clear responses in their pupils (Laeng et al. 2016)!

As the present book deals with animal emotions highly conserved in our human brain, we would like to approach the question of how music interacts with our ancient brain regions. First of all, there has been quite a lot of (admittedly academic) discussion on the nature of music. It's so difficult to define music that some scientists just leave it as follows: "You know it's music when you hear it." Moreover, it has been argued that music could represent an archaic prototypic language that happened to help our ancestors communicate before we were able to produce the complex sounds involved in our modern speech (Mithen 2009). This idea may live on in the typical mother–baby sing-a-long communication. Clearly, these melodic sounds, together with the warm touch of the mother, have a maximal soothing effect on a baby and calm the activity in the emotional circuitries for negative affect. I (CM) also know this from singing Rio Reiser's "Junimond" to my daughter each night, which soothes her into sleep. Here, I experience the real power of music! But not only babies and young children profit from these effects; adults benefit as well. Several MRI studies have been conducted showing that pleasant music triggers the brain areas of the SEEKING system, which cognitive neuroscientists would likely label the "reward system" (Montag, Reuter, and Axmacher 2011; Mueller et al. 2015). Music is not only rewarding, but energizes us and activates our emotions. Again, this explains why many professional athletes practice with music. Moreover, additional evidence comes from our own neuroimaging studies, showing that one's own favorite music, in particular, might be able to trigger the SEEKING system and provide us with positive energy. In discussing personality in Chapter 2, we mentioned that the SEEKING system might underlie the complex trait Openness for Experience. Fittingly, it has been repeatedly shown that people scoring high on this personality trait report feeling chills more often while listening to music (McCrae 2007). These people seem to be very receptive to the gifts music can give to us.

With this kind of information in mind, we want to touch briefly on the area of music therapy. This is a wide field of research of its own and here we are only considering the question: Is music able to down regulate pain? Indeed, this research question has been illuminated by evidence showing that music – and again one's own favorite music works best – might be able to reduce pain while being treated in the dentist's chair or after a person has undergone surgery (Bernatzky et al. 2011). So, next time, make sure to bring along your favorite music and ask the dentist to put it on! On a neurochemical level, the pain-alleviating effects of music might be, in part, mediated by endogenous opioids, which our brain produces as a consequence of listening to the music and which can also down regulate psychic pain (SADNESS circuitry) or physical pain.

Summary

Music is omnipresent in everyday life. This is for good reason, because music impacts our mood by interacting with our ancient animal emotions. If you want to down regulate your negative feelings in particular, your favorite (happy) music might help. A final thought not covered in this chapter should not be overlooked – music might simply simulate having social company when we are feeling alone. It's like turning on the TV to have some background chatter when we are alone; it may help us deal with our emotional pain when feeling lonely.

ANGER

I was in a taxi, on my way to the panda camp in Chengdu. Before getting into the taxi, I asked the taxi driver, in my (unfortunately) poor Mandarin, if he knew the way to the camp. Chengdu is famous for the panda breeding camp and a lot of Chinese tourists love to go there. They are all keen to see the cute panda babies.

Traffic in China is always an adventure. Nevertheless, in my many travels through the country, I have always felt safe, perhaps with the exception of this one day, in that taxi to the panda camp. The trip usually takes twenty to thirty minutes from my apartment. With this taxi driver, it took ninety minutes and he stopped several times on the highway to ask farmers for directions. The longer I sat in the taxi, the angrier I got, because the taxi driver was clearly cheating me. Let us not forget that he originally claimed to know the way. As an absolute highlight, he turned around on the highway, having come to the conclusion that we were obviously going the wrong way. Then we drove for several minutes on the wrong side of the highway, in danger of meeting oncoming traffic head on (no joke!). You can imagine that my brain activity at that moment was not only fueled by ANGER, but also by FEAR that we might end up in a bad accident.

When we finally arrived at the panda camp, the taxi driver demanded the full fare for the ninety-minute ride with all its many detours. This made me even angrier. I only paid half the price and mentioned that I would get the police, which then made him ANGRY. In the end, he just took the money and I got out of the car as fast as I could.

7

Of Animal Emotions and the Happy Life

"Of all the things which wisdom provides to make us entirely
happy, much the greatest is the possession of friendship."
— Epicurus

Which country is happiest? Well, according to data from the
Happy Planet Index (HPI), many industrialized and rich countries such as the U.S. or Germany are not really happy, to judge
by their rankings in a list of 140 countries. In fact, the contrary
seems to be true. The United States of America is ranked 108th.
Germany ranks a bit higher, but still not great at 49th. In contrast, surprising results can be spotted in the top ten of this list:
Here, you will find Colombia in the third spot, Mexico in the
second one and Costa Rica coming in first. These top three happiest countries are followed by Vanuatu in fourth and Vietnam
in the fifth position. Who would have guessed this order?

A closer look at the methods used to arrive at these results illu-
minates how this surprising ranking occurred. According to the
Happy Planet Index website, the HPI is calculated by multiply-
ing the self-reported (hence subjective) well-being measure of the
country's residents by their life-expectancy and by the inequality
of well-being/life expectancy within the group of residents in
the investigated country. This number is then divided by the
ecological footprint, a measure assessing the renewable resources
and CO_2 emissions required to support the country's residents
(Happy Planet Index 2016). Of special interest for our book on

animal emotions is the *subjective well-being measure* of the HPI. Here, humans are asked to indicate on a scale ranging from 0–10 how satisfied they are with their lives. Higher scores indicate higher life satisfaction. Although the use of the variable *overall life satisfaction*[1] represents an important part of well-being/happiness research, it only provides us with a limited and likely more cognitive view on this topic.

Ed Diener may be the most consistent contributor to the study of well-being, along with his frequent collaborator Richard Lucas. In one of their seminal works (2003), Diener, Scollon, and Lucas summarize that a full picture of subjective well-being/happiness can only emerge through the inclusion of information in four areas of subjective well-being: two affective, and two cognitive (see Figure 7.1). Notably, the term happiness is hard to define, but given its importance in general public discourse, we also use it somewhat interchangeably with the term *subjective well-being*.[2]

According to the Diener article, we need to take into account the two cognitive well-being facets to understand if a person is really happy. In short, humans are asked how satisfied they are with their lives overall ("Global" in Figure 7.1), as well as questions dealing with their specific life domains, such as *leisure activities, family,* or *work* ("Domain" in Figure 7.1). In a recent study by Lachmann et al. (2018), we observe that, in Germany in particular, satisfaction with one's own leisure activities was the best predictor of life satisfaction. Further, it should be mentioned that just adding up satisfaction levels of several life domains does *not* result in the overall life satisfaction of a person, because humans state different life domains to be of different importance to them. As a consequence, one would need to weigh each domain item before it could be added up, and it is not likely that all relevant life domains could be covered in a survey attempting to measure the overall life satisfaction of every person investigated.

1   Similar to the aforementioned 0–10 scale.
2   For further information on the origins of happiness research starting with the ancient Greek philosopher (Democritus) and problems in defining happiness, we refer to the cited work of Ed Diener.

Subjective Well-Being			
Positive Primary Emotions	Negative Primary Emotions	Global Life Judgement	Domain Satisfaction
SEEKING	FEAR	LIFE SATISFACTION	MARRIAGE
LUST	RAGE		HEALTH
CARE	SADNESS		WORK
PLAY			LEISURE
			INCOME

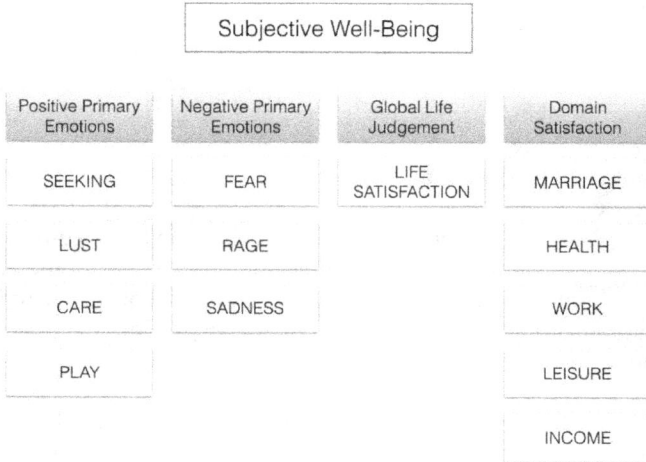

Fig. 7.1 A model of subjective well-being/happiness adapted from Diener et al. (2003, 192) and modified according to our thoughts in the present chapter

The other large component in this happiness research model considers an emotional approach to studying the well-being complex. Here, human participants give researchers insights into their recently experienced positive and negative emotions. This indicates, as with the satisfaction measures, that well-being is not a stable trait, but fluctuates over one's life. Aside from this fact, humans with a certain kind of personality structure tend to show higher or lower life satisfaction over the course of their lives. For example, neurotic people tend to more often report lower life satisfaction, and extraverted people report higher life satisfaction.[3]

A survey covering the emotional aspects of well-being would ask about positive emotions, such as how much laughing, smiling and enjoyment a person has recently experienced in his/her life. Naturally, participants in the survey would also need to be

3   See also Chapter 2 on personality and animal emotions for an introduction to the psychological constructs of personality; also, see the aforementioned work by Lachmann et al. (2018).

asked about negative emotions, such as how much they worried or how much anger/sadness was being experienced in their lives. Of tremendous interest, the emotional domains of well-being research originally presented in the Diener paper strongly overlap with many of the emotional terms used to describe animal emotions in the present book. In their article, Diener, Scollon, and Lucas (2003) use the terms "sadness, anger, worry, stress" as examples of unpleasant emotions, and the terms "joy, contentment, happiness, love" as examples of positive emotions. As these feelings arise from the activity of primal emotional neural networks deeply anchored in our brains, we presented the seven animal emotions as discussed in the present book instead of the original terms used by Diener in Figure 7.1.

In sum, Diener's work on happiness/well-being not only considers cognitive facets, but also emotional facets to understand well-being. In order to be truly happy, one needs, on the one hand, high overall life satisfaction and high satisfaction in several domains of life. On the other hand, a more positive emotional experience, together with fewer experienced negative affects, would typically be reported by a happy person.

Returning to the previously mentioned results from the HPI, we would like to briefly shed some light on the links between happiness and income. For quite some time, it has been put forward in the psycho-economic literature that the association between emotional well-being and yearly income is not strictly linear. Instead, a certain amount of money is needed to achieve a certain amount of emotional well-being, whereas surpassing such an amount of yearly income is not followed by a further increase in emotional well-being. Meanwhile, so-called *Happiness Income Benchmarks* have been established. These describe thresholds of U.S. dollar income per year; that is, thresholds above which "happiness" does not further increase. The *Huffington Post* website (Short 2017) depicts a map of the U.S. showing that earning, for example, more than $65,850 U.S. dollars a year in the state of Mississippi does not lead to further increases in emotional well-being. These numbers were based on a study by Nobel Prize laureate Daniel Kahnemann and his colleague Angus Deaton. Their study demonstrated that, across the U.S., an income higher than $75,000 U.S. dollars did not result in a higher increment of emotional well-being.[4] In contrast, the cognitive facet of well-being/happiness (hence overall life satisfaction) seems to increase further with higher income (Kahneman and Deaton 2010).

Despite the interesting links between income and well-being, many other factors beyond income must also play an important role in fully understanding happiness. Otherwise, one could not explain why countries comparably poorer than the U.S. or Germany are leading the list of countries in the HPI. Simply living in a rich country (or having lots of money for oneself) does not lead to a super happy life, particularly when it comes to the emotional aspects of happiness. Somehow, it seems that many countries with far fewer economic resources are better able to take care of their basic needs, understood as those needs arising from our animal emotions.

In line with these insights, the importance of economic pathways to well-being is being challenged in our modern times. This was already emphasized in 1972 in a small country in the Himalayan region. Druk Gyalpo, the fourth Dragon King of Bhutan, decided to measure the success of his country by relying upon an index called *gross national happiness* (instead of relying on the common gross national product). By this he meant that becoming and staying happy represents the most important goal for the citizens of his country. That might, in part, explain why Bhutan is often described as the happiest nation in the world, although this is challenged by its ranking as 56th on the HPI. Nevertheless, one can ask why an economically poor country such as Bhutan has a better position than the United States of America on the HPI. Perhaps we may find an answer in the high spirituality of the Drukpa[5] (who mostly follow a Buddhist lifestyle) and their strong family bonds, together with a strong sense of CAREing for each other. Finally, they live in a wonderful, green, Himalayan environment. It is well known that mega-cities with their loudness and environmental pollution exert a great deal of

---

4 A more recent work by Kushlev, Dunn, and Lucas (2015) is also highly interesting, providing evidence that higher income might be better at reducing sadness, instead of enhancing happiness.

5 The residents of Bhutan call themselves the *Drukpa* or "dragon people."

stress on their inhabitants, which also results in higher suscep-
tibility to mental disorders such as schizophrenia (Vassos et al.
2012). However, we would nevertheless like to point to recent
work from Christian's group that unexpectedly shows that growing up in urban areas has a (very small) positive effect on shaping
primary emotions: For females, growing up in (Chinese) urban
mega-cities was associated with lower FEAR/SADNESS scores
on the *Affective Neuroscience Personality Scales* in adulthood,
whereas in males, it was associated with higher PLAY scores. For
more detail, please see the paper by Sindermann et al. (2017).

Druk Gyalpo's idea to put happiness – hence psychic well-
being – on the political agenda is revolutionary compared to
our ever more hectic and stressful lives in industrially developed
Western countries, as well as in some Eastern countries such as
Japan and China. Interestingly, the founders of the United States
of America had formulated similar thoughts much earlier, when
they envisioned the right of every American citizen to *the pursuit
of happiness*. This is something that we might need to remember
and consider more often in an accelerating, globalized world,
increasingly dominated by technological revolutions.

In order to focus more closely in this chapter on the primary
emotional systems, we provide the reader with some new unpublished data sets from our group, in which participants filled in
the *Affective Neuroscience Personality Scales – Adjective Ratings*
(ANPS-AR) to assess individual differences in primary emotional
traits and overall life satisfaction (see Table 7.1). We see a pattern: positive emotions (SEEKING, CARE, PLAY) are positively
linked to overall life satisfaction and negative emotions (FEAR,
SADNESS, ANGER) are inversely linked to overall life satisfaction.

To readers unfamiliar with statistics, the r (a correlation coef-
ficient) can range between -1 and $+1$. The more positive the r,
the stronger the positive association between two variables.
For example, the taller a person, the more they weigh. Negative
numbers would indicate, in our case, that higher negative emotionality goes along with lower overall life satisfaction. Numbers
around zero speak for no association between two investigated
variables. One of the problems of using correlations is the fact
that they do not give insights into causal mechanisms underly-

ing a potential association. Hence correlations cannot answer: Which came first, the chicken or the egg?

In the context of our present data, it is noteworthy that primary emotional systems as assessed by the ANPS are known to be fairly stable[6] and life satisfaction measures are known to fluctuate more. As a consequence, it is likely that individual differences in primary emotional trait system levels (seen as a relatively stable disposition to act more or less in a certain way) influence overall life satisfaction.[7] Ergo, our emotional traits arising from our ancient animal neural circuitries likely influence the cognitive facets of well-being. Along these lines, we collected data from 3,976 people from the general population (2,414 males and 1,562 females; mean age: 32.40 with a standard deviation of 12.12) via a German website investigating, among other things, technology use and personality. Here, participants filled out a slightly different German short version of the English ANPS-AR[8] as well as Diener's 5-item well-being scale (see upper half of Table 7.1 below). The second sample in the lower half of Table 7.1 consisted of 4,049 English speaking gamers (1,942 males and 2,107 females; mean age: 26.88 with a standard deviation of 7.26) who filled in the English version of the ANPS-AR together with one item assessing life satisfaction/subjective happiness taken from a longer scale as presented in Lyubomirsky and Lepper (1999). This gamer sample is characterized in more detail in the self-test appendix, where you will also find the English version of the ANPS-AR alongside data against which you can compare yourself. In general, we believe both samples to be of interest, because data were collected online from the general population and not only from students. This is an important and frequent critique. It has even been said that most psychological research

6 Most people respond to questions in the ANPS in the same way they did four years ago when completing the questionnaire (Orri et al. 2018). Note that here version 2.4 of the ANPS was used.

7 Again, see Chapter 2, in which we indicate that the primary emotional traits influence personality bottom-up.

8 The English version of the ANPS-AR as published in Montag and Davis (2018) is presented in the Appendix. Note, however, that a four Likert scale was used in the German sample.

	SEEKING	CARE	PLAY	FEAR	ANGER	SADNESS
Subjective Well-Being	r = .46, p < .001	r = .17, p < .001	r = .12, p < .001	r = −.43, p < .001	r = −.11, p < .001	r = −.48, p < .001
Subjective Happiness Measure	r = .32, p < .001	r = .18, p < .001	r = .25, p < .001	r = −.47, p < .001	r = −.14, p < .001	r = −.57, p < .001

Table 7.1: Positive primary emotional systems are linked positively to life satisfaction/subjective well-being, and negative primary emotional systems are negatively linked to life satisfaction/subjective well-being. Although the results appear to be highly robust, see these results from the upper half as preliminary. (The German version of the ANPS-AR used in this study in the upper half is still undergoing psychometric testing and will need to be further improved.) For the cognitive facet of Subjective Well-Being, life satisfaction was assessed with a scale developed by Diener et al. (1985). For the Subjective Happiness Measure, we assessed life satisfaction with one item from the Subjective Happiness Scale by Lyubomirsky and Lepper (1999).

is carried out on WEIRD participants (Henrich, Heine, and Norenzayan 2010). This acronym describes participants usually stemming from Western parts of the world, being Educated with an Industrialized, Rich, and Democratic background.

Participants in the sample recruited from the general German-speaking population presented in the upper half of Table 7.1 reported high well-being (M = 24.86 with a standard deviation of 6.15; the lowest score could be 5 and the highest score on this well-being scale was 35). The English-speaking sample in the lower half of the Table scored a mean of 4.87 points (standard deviation: 1.50) on the life satisfaction item ranging from 1–7. Answer option 1 means "In general, I consider myself *not* a very happy person" and answer option 7 means "In general, I consider myself a very happy person." Contrasting the results from the upper and bottom halves in Table 7.1, it becomes apparent that correlations are highly consistent. This is noteworthy, as the life satisfaction measures differed. The observation that positive primary emotions are positively linked to well-being, and negative primary emotions are inversely linked to well-being, appears to be quite robust. The most pronounced effects can be observed for SEEKING (+), FEAR (−), and SADNESS (−), with correlations all about .30 or higher. In general, we believe it safe to conclude that taking care of one's needs linked to the positive and negative primary emotions seems a good way to heighten one's own well-being and life satisfaction. While this data is not causally linked to outcomes, there are hints that the anxieties associated with physical dangers (FEAR) and the anxieties associated with social separation distress (SADNESS) are likely to limit one's capacity to experience positive emotions.

Taking a further look at the correlations, we also find it interesting that the trait PLAYfulness is positively associated with overall life satisfaction (notably much stronger in the lower half of Table 7.1). This positive association also makes sense in the light of the earlier presented data stating that: a) PLAY influences extraversion bottom-up and; b) extraversion is positively linked to life satisfaction. Unfortunately, we know that PLAY behavior is fragile. Humans (children in particular) play when no danger is near and the human mind is in a positive mood. As Jaak Panksepp reported in his book *Affective Neuroscience* (1998), and as his student Stephen Siviy, working with his own students, later expanded upon (Siviy, Harrison, and McGregor 2006) there is animal research evidence supporting this observation. The presence of cat hair (instinctively eliciting FEAR) was enough to stop the play behavior of rats that had never experienced a cat, showing a strong link between the PLAY and FEAR systems, which supports the idea presented above that negative primary emotions can interfere with the experience of positive emotions. Initiating PLAY behavior in order to achieve higher well-being is a good strategy to enhance well-being. However, in a fearful emotional mindset, PLAY activity will likely not be observable. PLAY also decreases if one of the partners becomes too aggressive and starts winning all the time. And, although difficult to test, "homesick" puppies taken away from their homes and their littermates are not likely to be eager playmates. However, it would be difficult to test with young puppies because they are so resilient and will soon start playing with children and even adults if other puppies are not around. This animal research is also reflected in the negative correlations between all negative emotional systems and overall life satisfaction.

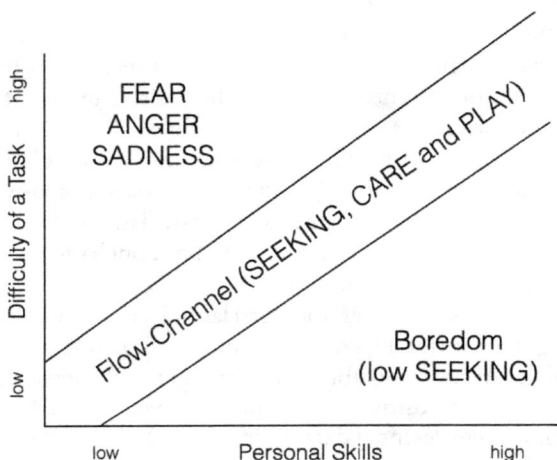

Fig. 7.2 Primary emotions and Csikszentmihalyi (2008, 74)'s flow concept: theoretical assumptions.

The last section of this chapter about well-being and animal emotions deals with a famous construct called *flow* from the realm of positive psychology. As mentioned in an earlier chapter, the psychologist Mihaly Csikszentmihalyi introduced this concept (Csikszentmihalyi 2008). Flow describes a state of mind in which we are totally focused on an activity, which could be anything from climbing a mountain, becoming immersed in the latest computer game, a deep conversation with a beloved person, but also work (yes!). While in the "zone," in the flow channel, we forget about time and space. In order to understand how we can get into the flow channel, we provide you with Figure 7.2, which we explain in the following paragraphs.

As depicted in the figure adapted from Czikszentmihalyi's work, one sees that a perfect match between one's own abilities and the difficulty of a task define the flow channel. To explain this: Imagine yourself being new at a job. In the beginning, things might be a bit overwhelming, leading, in the worst case scenario, to activity in the FEAR circuitry (FEARing you won't excel in the job), SADNESS circuitry (not satisfied with your performance and concerned about critical rejection from peers and supervisor), or ANGER (if you have the feeling of being treated unfairly on the job or being frustrated by your failure). Hence, activity in our negative primary animal emotions is likely when our skills do not match the difficulty of the task.

Now imagine yourself having done the same job for years. Nothing has changed in your daily work routine. You know every aspect of what to do, starting from 9 a.m. to the end of the workday at 5 p.m. This "being under-challenged" leads ultimately to boredom (an under-arousal of the SEEKING system), which also kills the flow experience. Again, we are not in the zone! So where can our positive animal emotions be anchored in the flow model now?

As being in the flow channel represents a very positive state of mind in which we work through things with ease, it is obvious that enthusiasm stemming from activity in the SEEKING and PLAY systems is likely happening in the flow zone. Given that different settings where flow can happen are possible (e.g., an intimate discussion with a beloved person), it is also imaginable that the CARE circuitry might be activated in the flow zone, but only in social settings. We explicitly mention that the thoughts proposed here about associations between primary emotions and flow are of a theoretical nature and need to backed up by empirical findings.

Considering the needs arising from our heritage of animal emotions in our modern times: what makes us happy? Before exploring the answer through Pankseppian AN theory, we would like to briefly revisit an often cited theory called Maslow's "hierarchy of needs" (Maslow 1943). According to the study of biographies of prominent and highly successful people, Maslow came up with the idea of his pyramid (see Figure 7.3, left side). You have probably stumbled upon it already in a textbook, as it is still very popular in many disciplines.

Maslow argued that the lower needs of the pyramid have to be fulfilled first, before higher needs can be satisfied. Hence, only after meeting the needs of hunger and thirst can a person strive to satisfy the next higher need: safety. The higher you go up on the ladder, the more cognitive in nature the needs are. According to Maslow's early version of his theory, the highest goal to be achieved would be self-actualization. This means that to become a truly happy – here satisfied – person, one has to live up to one's

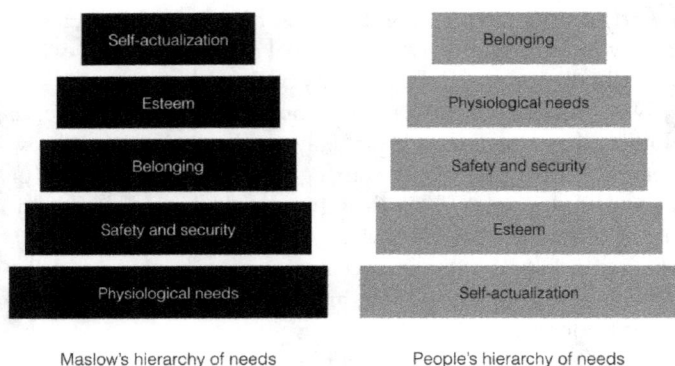

Fig. 7.3 Maslow's ideal hierarchy of needs compared to the hierarchy of needs stated by $N = 850$ participants (210 males and 640 females; $M_{age} = 37.04$ years, $SD_{age} = 14.59$ years).

own full potential. In as yet unpublished data, we observed that higher scores in FEAR and SADNESS as emotional personality traits seem to counteract fulfillment of all of Maslow's needs, whereas higher scores in PLAY might be helpful to fulfill the different needs presented in Maslow's pyramid.[9] What we found most interesting was the answer given by the participants about the importance of each of Maslow's needs in their lives. Here they were asked to rank the five terms in an order of 1 to 5, with 1 being of lowest importance and 5 of highest importance. As you can see from the alternative pyramid resulting from the empirical data of this study (Figure 7.3 on the right side), self-actualization was ranked last on the pyramid by the participants, whereas belonging and safety came in first. We believe that these data support Jaak's theory and show how our evolutionary heritage strongly resonates within us. Despite our cognitive abilities, we are emotional beings influenced by primary emotional systems.

According to Jaak, finding happiness might be simply answered with the following: Engage more in SEEKING (energetic exploration of the world, which is why a lot of people love

9 Please note that the study is of correlational nature.

to travel), CARE and PLAY. Notably, both CAREing for others and being CAREd for feel good. Particularly important is the power of touch; being embraced by your beloved partner is a wonderful experience that down regulates SADness. The same is true for engaging in PLAY behavior. Again, this is a joyful activity we are sharing with another PLAY partner. Hence, social interactions are a tremendous driver for experiencing happiness. Let's not forget that we are social animals in need of companionship. Clearly, understanding our primary-process animal emotions is key to understanding ourselves.

Summary

The study of well-being is complex and many approaches have been taken to understand what makes us happy. The present chapter argues that taking care of our ancestral emotional heritage is ultimately the key to happiness and well-being.

So again, what makes us happy? It's the energy derived from the activity of the SEEKING system (enthusiasm), the soothing effects of CAREing for each other (feelings of tenderness and comfort), and the joy of PLAYing with one another. Engaging these pleasant primary emotions may also need to be augmented by the absence (or down regulation) of activity in the aversive primary brain systems: FEAR, ANGER, and SADNESS.

Finally, happiness is multi-faceted and can result from quite different affective experiences. In short: romantic love (LUST), parental love (CARE), experiencing joyous fun (PLAY), and engaging in a favorite interest or exploring a challenging problem (SEEKING), are four of the basic pleasures in our mammalian lives. Note that sensory affects (smelling the roses) can be associated with improved well-being, as in aromatherapy and the use of perfumes. Perhaps more fundamental to happiness, homeostatic affects such as hunger or thirst can be stilled via activity of the SEEKING system. Consuming a drink or food when thirsty or hungry is clearly also pleasurable, but note that these urges are also fulfilled by the common activation of the motivational SEEKING system.

PLAY

I rang the bell at my brother's house. After a short wait, the door opened and my five-year-old nephew was standing there smiling at me. "Hello Christian!" he said, and his smile grew bigger. I went to grab him. As a consequence, he ran into the living room and I followed him as fast as I could. He laughed joyfully when I began to chase him. From the living room, he ran into the kitchen and hid behind the kitchen table. The longer the chase went on, the more joyful his laughter became. After two minutes, I caught and tickled him. He bounced into my arms and could not stop laughing.

. . . . books . . . a short walk to the door,
opened . . . carefully . . . time, wondering how smiling
along . . . wall . . . and he to remember. I
worried . . . it . . . that . . . through . . . his sort
. . . . with . . . shed, though I
been to . . . and . . . thought it . . . be in terror . . . at
as his . . . . massive one
the first . . . . lamp
went right . . . . turned . . .
. . .

8

Affective Neuroscience Theory and Other Approaches to Understanding Emotions

"Acquire new knowledge whilst thinking over the old, and you
may become a teacher of others."
— Confucius

The present publication centers on AN theory. To the layperson, the discussion so far might appear as if no other prominent theories exist for categorizing emotions. This is far from true. Many important scholars have shaped the study of emotions, and we cannot present them all here. Indeed, Jaak's work has not only been strongly influenced by Charles Darwin's theory of evolution (as featured in the personality section in Chapter 2) but also by Paul MacLean's studies of cross-species brain evolution, his best-known book being *The Triune Brain in Evolution: Role in Paleocerebral Functions* (1990). Following Darwin's work studying emotions and facial expressions across species – in humans and other mammals – Paul Ekman has focused on gaining insights into the emotional states of a person by reading his or her face (Ekman, Friesen, and Ellsworth 2013). In the last decades, Ekman and his colleagues have done numerous detailed studies on human facial expressions in search of human personality universals. Through his research, Ekman has sought to identify universal facial expressions that are independent of the cultural backgrounds of the people both interpreting and producing those facial expressions. While there are similarities to those affects identified in Jaak's AN theory, Ekman comes to slightly different categories of emotion. Aside from fearful, angry, and sad, which obviously find matches with Panksepp's taxonomy of negative affects, Ekman's joyful facial expression may arise from activity in different positive primal emotional neural circuits, although Panksepp's first choice would likely have been PLAY. Ekman additionally describes the facial expressions of disgust, surprise and contempt.

Why are there differences between the two theories? In a recent paper, Jaak and Christian wrote that "the study of facial expression as well as other emotional action patterns represents the preeminent scientific human-behavioral pattern entry point to this important research topic from the outside perspective, while mapping the primal circuitry underlying emotions provides a scientific view from the inside" (Montag and Panksepp 2016, 761). So, different approaches might result in different taxonomies; however, a strong point can be made for globally valid emotions, when the same lists are derived using different methods. Therefore, Panksepp and Ekman both observing FEAR, ANGER, and SADNESS clearly speaks for a valid global taxonomy of negative emotional affects. Further, Ekman's joyfulness facial expression could be linked to SEEKING or PLAY, but the full "Duchenne smile" – the big smile usually used to identify this facial expression – is more likely linked with PLAY and its associated laughter.

This said, as stated in a 2016 paper by Montag and Panksepp, we see problems viewing surprise, disgust, or contempt as distinct emotional expressions, in particular when characterizing them as primary-process raw emotional affects. The case of surprise has been discussed earlier and we all know of examples in which we can be surprised without the need for a particular emotional content accompanying the event surprising us (think of the Beijing example at the beginning of the book). Regarding disgust, Panksepp has written many times that disgust is likely better categorized as a sensory affect reflecting the need to spit something disgusting (dis + gustatory) out of one's mouth or perhaps reacting to some creepy-crawly thing on one's skin that needs to be removed as soon as possible.

If surprise and disgust have recognizable facial expressions, the other side of the debate might ask why one of the most prototypical primary emotions, namely the CARE system, is not associated with a distinct facial expression. In their study of the ability of persons to detect facial expressions such as disgust, Widen et al. (2011) found that only few of their 148 subjects could accurately label a face designed to display "compassion," likely representing a CAREing person. Such issues cast doubt on whether facial expressions are a sufficient criterion to identify primary emotional brain action systems. This said, CARE is a positive primary emotion and might be linked to the joyful/happy facial expression (Montag and Panksepp 2016).

Originally, Ekman and Friesen (1971) only reported six universal facial expressions: anger, fear, sadness, happiness, surprise, and disgust. Later, Ekman and Heider (1988) added a seventh candidate: contempt. However, in contrast to the previous list of six universals, "contempt" did not receive "universal" acceptance by the psychological community. Even Ekman's own research did not confirm the robust results for contempt that he and others had reported for the original six (Matsumoto and Ekman 2004). A facial expression of contempt is also not included in Panksepp's list of primary-process emotions, derived from cross-species research. It likely arises from complex interactions between primal emotions and activity of evolutionarily more recently developed brain layers. In the 2016 Montag and Panksepp paper, we hypothesized that contempt might result from the energy of both the disgust and ANGER circuitry. However, contempt is not a hotheaded state. Therefore, prefrontally steered emotional regulation activity is probably needed to give rise to this cognitive (emotional) facial expression. Beyond that, Fischer and Giner-Sorolla (2016) nicely describe the way in which contempt both overlaps with and differs from the ANGER circuitry. In their view, ANGER is elicited when we consider other people to be transgressing morally accepted norms. In this light, it is also interesting that Christian's group linked higher ANGER to higher and more cognitive vengefulness (Sindermann et al. 2018). Beyond that, Fischer and Giner-Sorolla (2016) argue: "Unlike anger, contempt arises when a person's or group's character is appraised as bad and unresponsive to change, leading to attempts to socially exclude the target" (346). Still, we believe that contempt, like hate and vengefulness, represents a cognitive refinement of primary ANGER.

Finally, because humans have the capability to influence their emotional facial expression, e.g., by putting on a smiling face although feeling bad, Paul Ekman found ways to detect such fake expressions in the human face. In short, fake versus genuine emotional expressions can be exposed due to slightly altered muscle groups involved in the production of facial expressions.

However, new experiments have challenged the idea of the universality of some of Ekman's facial expressions by introducing a simple change to the original experimental setup (Widen et al. 2011). Usually, Ekman's faces are presented with words describing the depicted emotions. The participants of an experiment then need to pick the correct word for the presented facial expression (these words function as verbal cues or suggestions). If the experiment is conducted this way, users are pretty good at this task. This would speak for the generalizability of basic emotions. But, when there is only an open question presented ("What is the depicted emotion called?"), without including a verbal cue, there is more room for interpretation and the universality of the participants' responses goes down (but only for facial expressions such as contempt or shame (not discussed here); hence, those going beyond the original basic emotions). From our point of view, it is generally questionable whether simply recognizing emotions (from a purely external perspective) will, in the end, help to sufficiently answer the question as to the existence of basic emotions, because facial expressions are a complicated mix of energy being fueled by many brain areas.

Beyond the important work of Paul Ekman, other important theorists need to be named, such as Carroll Izard, who also worked on facial expressions and is known for his Differential Emotion Theory (DET) (Izard and Buechler 1980). In short, Izard described three issues at the core of DET, which also fit with Panksepp's AN theory. First, independent basic emotions exist (in his theory: joy, interest, anger, fear, sadness, surprise, and disgust). "Independent" means that the activation of these emotional systems does not rely on the cognitive development of the brain (an idea that was championed for years by Silvan

Tompkins, who was a mentor to both Ekman and Izard) or on psychological mechanisms such as cognitive appraisal. Second, emotions should be discrete. In line with Ekman's work, this means that specific muscular activities underlie each emotion. This activity might differ in its expressive strength depending on a given situation's level of evolutionary significance. Being attacked by a wild animal would end up in a full-blown facial FEAR expression, whereas worrying might result in a milder facial expression of FEAR. Third, these emotions should be stable across the development of humans (for more detail, see Ackerman, Abe, and Izard 1998). Finally, another bridge can be built between Izard's DET and the 2016 paper by Montag and Panksepp, as presented in the chapter on personality: "Emotion thresholds differ among individuals, as does the intensity of a feeling state when an emotion is activated" (98).

Aside from Ekman and Izard, we would briefly like to mention James Russell, whose work on emotions was compared and contrasted with Panksepp's work in a book-length volume called *Categorical versus Dimensional Models of Affect* (Zachar and Ellis 2012). Unique among the personality/emotion theorists discussed up to this point, Russell traces all discrete emotions back to two basic fundamental axes referred to as the "dimensions" of (pleasant/unpleasant) valence and (low/high) arousal. This approach belongs to a psychological constructivist's view on emotion, challenging the concept of "discrete categories" of basic emotions as presented in this book, because it states that all emotions are concepts derived from socio-developmental learning and every emotion can be labeled on the two aforementioned dimensional axes. E.g., I interpret my current high arousal and high negative affect FEAR due to seeing a snake. Such an interpretation would rely heavily on neocortical processes – also in the realm of primary emotional systems.

For us personally, this approach to understanding primary emotions does not fit well with what we observe in the neuroscientific data. A major argument for Jaak's theory is the finding that, even after decortication of young mammals (meaning the recent evolutionary layer that is less developed than in humans has been surgically removed), animal emotions are still readily observed. Indeed, it can be difficult to say with confidence which animals have had the surgery. For example, consider the case of decorticate rats PLAYing (Panksepp et al. 1994). Hence, animal emotions must reside in the more ancient subcortical brain areas rather than being a neocortical function. Also supporting Jaak's view on basic emotions is that distinct emotional action patterns can be observed with Deep Brain Stimulation (DBS) in corresponding ancient brain areas in animals. Earlier, we acknowledged that more complex emotions such as shame or guilt rely on activity of more recently developed brain layers.

It should be noted that the approaches of Jaak Panksepp and James Russell could be brought together. First of all, Panksepp's theory allowed for neocortical cognitive influences, including sustaining emotional arousal as well as down regulating it. His theory also conceived of primary emotions as learning systems that allowed learning from our emotional experiences to alter the expression of our emotions. However, where Panksepp and the psychological construction theorists such as Russell might have difficulty resolving their differences would be in acknowledging that primary emotional systems are also the foundation of our emotional experiences in each emotional situation. This important difference is not easily glossed over. Among the most difficult issues to resolve is that learning is not required for the expression of discrete emotion systems such as FEAR and PLAY, which Russell would regard as requiring cognitive construction involving language. Further, as already alluded to, total elimination of neocortical regions at birth leaves all the discrete emotions intact, with further evidence being that human children born without a cortex also exhibit a range of discrete primary emotions (Solms and Panksepp 2012). In contrast, when subcortical regions are damaged in animals and humans, emotional capacities are severely compromised.

However, as Jaak Panksepp has argued

A primary process/basic emotion view may prevail in many subcortical regions, and constructivist/dimensional approaches may effectively parse higher emotional concepts as processed by the neocortex [...]. In other words, such debates may simply reflect investigators working at different levels of control. (Panksepp 2010, 536)

As already mentioned in the present work, we are seldom so overwhelmed by our built-in genetic emotional systems that we feel the most raw affect in its purest form, but everyone knows how it feels to have a heated argument. We are aligned with Jaak Panksepp that our view on emotions will be enriched when one includes both the social developmental view of emotions envisioned by Russell and the evolutionary/genetic primary foundation of emotions that Panksepp has so clearly documented. The latter refers to the concepts of basic emotions or primary emotional systems in the present work. It is more than likely that when being attacked by a lion in the savannah, typical fight, flight, freezing behavior will be elicited without further need of cognitive appraisal. In such a situation, there is simply no room for constructing an emotion. Due to ethical reasons, such situations of evolutionary significance are often problematic to study in humans or other mammals, in particular when dealing with negative animal emotions.[1]

Again, for a recent (and detailed) discussion on Jaak and Russell's work, see a very interesting work by Zachar and Ellis (2012) presenting arguments for both Panksepp's and Russell's views on emotions. This said, Russell's dimensional approach to emotions can be used to locate each of Panksepp's emotions descriptively on the dimensions of valence and arousal: e.g., FEAR could be described with high unpleasant valence and high arousal. SEEKING would be characterized by high arousal and high positive valence. But maybe these descriptions are, in the end, too broad to clearly distinguish between different kinds of positive/negative emotions as mapped with electrical brain stimulation. Moreover, this is just a descriptive way of bringing the theories together, and Russell's view on emotions provides no insight into the foundation of human emotions in the brain. Nevertheless, in the 2012 Zachar and Ellis book noted above, an optimistic Panksepp wrote:

> I think this [reconciling the two approaches] could be achieved if CA [Core Affect] theory[2] were simply cast as a

---

1 But see interesting imaging work by Mobbs et al. (2007).
2 Russell's view.

tertiary-process theory about the cortical aspects of higher-order human emotions, and not at all a theory of affective life across species. (317)

This said, many other important contributors to the study of emotion should be noted, such as Jeffrey Gray's pioneering work in the investigation of behavioral activation and inhibition systems (basic approach and avoidance behavior). Also noteworthy are Walter Bradford Cannon, Sydney William Britton, and James Olds, all of whom were pioneers in electrical brain stimulation research. Naturally, in such a short introduction as the present one, we cannot go into more detail. It is crucial that the research fields build stronger bridges among all these theories in order to shape an ultimate theory of emotions. This is also something Jaak mentioned to me (CM) in an email on September 1, 2016, after our paper on Ekman's (and Jaak's) work was finally published: "Thanks for re-inspiring me to coax the field toward a more comprehensive synthesis." And earlier in this same email he noted: "As usual, a generation has to pass before the path is cleared for such syntheses."

We think it's time for my generation of scientists to get at such a synthesis, one in which there is meaningful consensus across theories.

Summary

The present book focuses on Panksepp's theory of Affective Neuroscience. However, the work of many other important scientists should be strongly considered in order to form a more detailed overview of what emotions are. This short chapter discusses, in particular, the example of Paul Ekman's famous work, but it also considers the constructivists and how a synergy between different theories can be achieved (at least in part). Aside from this, we are convinced that a focus on Panksepp's work justifies a volume of its own. Jaak's impact on psychology/psychiatry and its related disciplines will be felt for decades to come.

A Note from the Authors

Dear Reader,

We hope that you have enjoyed reading this brief introduction to Jaak Panksepp's rich lifetime achievement. If you were already familiar with Jaak's theory, we can only hope that you found something of relevance going beyond what you might have read in Jaak's main works, *Affective Neuroscience* and *The Archaeology of Mind*. We have focused this book on the AN theory as originally proposed by Jaak Panksepp. However, there are a great many talented scientists in the world studying the nature of emotions who have not been mentioned in this short volume. Writing this small volume clearly needed a focus, and perhaps other researchers would have chosen to do so in another way.

If you are interested in ongoing research using the *Affective Neuroscience Personality Scales,* we invite you to visit http://www.anps-research.com. There you will find not only information on relevant scientific papers, but also information on the availability of the ANPS in different languages.

We would like to deeply thank Eileen A. Joy from punctum books for her trust in this project. We are delighted to see our book become part of the punctum books catalogue. Moreover, we thank Vincent W.J. van Gerven Oei for providing us with the book design and last, but not least, Jessica Powell, for her work improving the readability of our book.

Finally, we thank Benjamin Becker, Markus Kiefer, Bernd Lachmann, Sebastian Markett, Halley Pontes, Martin Reuter, Dmitri Rozgonjuk, Rayna Sariyska, Helena Schmitt, Cornelia

Sindermann, Mareike Sittler, and Jennifer Wernicke for their support. They helped in different ways. You might have recognized that some of their names appeared in the book, because they conducted research we have written about. As mentioned, Martin introduced Christian to Jaak. Furthermore, Bernd, Dmitri, Helena, Cornelia, and Jennifer helped by checking the proofs and tables with the statistics provided in this book. Thanks are also due to the many participants, not mentioned here by name, who supported our studies and colleagues who collaborated with us.

Believe it or not, from the initial idea of this book in 2016, it took us four years to finish this project. Now it's done.

Sincerely yours,

Christian Montag & Kenneth L. Davis

Jaak and Christian in 2012 in Pullman.

Christian thanks...

I again thank Jaak for his support over the years. Without his great body of work, his enthusiasm, and creativity until his last days, the present book would not exist.

As also mentioned in the introduction, a big thanks goes to Ken for his support in finalizing this book. I could think of no one better to do it instead of Jaak. I am sure that Jaak would be delighted to see us collaborating on this project.

Finally, I thank my wife, Susanne, for being patient when I spend too much time writing at my computer. Although the present volume is a smaller one, it is my second popular science book, and writing always takes time. Hannah, my little girl, now you are in the world. Simply seeing you elicits strong CARE activity in my brain.

The last thanks go to my parents, Udo and Ingrid. They have been a great support for more than 40 years now! I also thank my brother, Thomas, for being a great friend. I am eager to go to the next soccer match of 1.FC Köln with him (where we will both enjoy drinking Kölsch).

For Christian's recent (research) activities, please visit http://www.christianmontag.de or Twitter: @ChrisMontag77.

Kenneth thanks...

I want to thank Christian for inviting me to join this project, and I look forward to future collaborations with him. My wife, Nancy, (who always seamlessly blends into our affective neuroscience travels) and I visited Christian, Susanne, and Hannah "where the Dom is" in Cologne for a few days in July, 2019. Hannah was a delight, and Susanne CAREingly dedicated her whole weekend to taking care of us. Altogether, the hospitality, the Kölsch, and the bratwurst (plus watching the Rhine light up at night during the Kölner Lichter celebration) all exceeded expectations. And yes, Susanne and Christian took us to see the magnificent Dom, the cathedral of Cologne.

I want to thank Nancy for not only tolerating the extra work I do for my various affective neuroscience projects, which sometimes leads to neglecting other things she would like me to do, but also for critically reading much of what I write and taking a real interest in Jaak and his wife, Anesa, who is a published author and who may (if we are lucky) write a book on her life with Jaak.

What can I say about Jaak that has not already been said? He became my anchor in graduate school and introduced me to an amazing neuroscience world that frequently required no statistics, because the effects on behavior so clearly separated the treated subjects from the controls (such as the dramatic influence of low doses of morphine and its short-term blocker naloxone on the social behavior of dogs). He also nonjudgmentally tolerated my disappearance into the business world and then welcomed me back with a series of projects, from developing the *Affective Neuroscience Personality Scales* to writing *The Emotional Foundations of Personality,* which, for me, became the equivalent of doing a postdoc, as I continued to learn from Jaak.

In the end, I see this book as part of an ongoing effort to promote what Jaak gave to the world: the most complete vision of humanity since Darwin, a vision that now neuroscientifically grounds our evolutionary mammalian heritage.

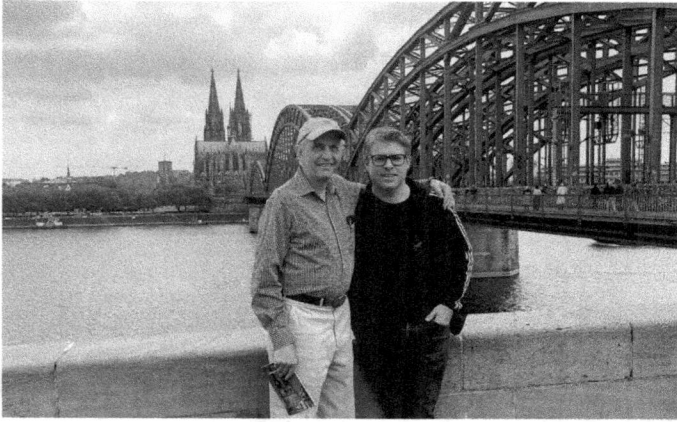

Ken and Christian in 2019 in Cologne, shortly before finalizing the book *Animal Emotions*

Affective Neuroscience
Personality Scales

Compare your emotional personality score with the emotional personality scores of others by completing the Affective Neuroscience Personality Scales

The *Affective Neuroscience Personality Scales* (ANPS) have been constructed to assess individual differences in primary emotional systems according to Pankseppian AN theory. Notably, such an approach comes with limitations, because primary emotional systems are located in subcortical regions of the brain and often operate at a subconscious level. By completing this assessment, you think about yourself and how these systems operate in you. Thus, assessing individual differences in primary emotional systems can only be a cognitive assessment of how you see your emotional personality.

There exist different versions of the *Affective Neuroscience Personality Scales,* such as the ANPS 2.4 presented in the book *The Emotional Foundations of Personality* by Davis and Panksepp (2018) and in the scientific paper by Davis and Panksepp (2011). The ANPS-AR (AR stands for adjective ratings), included below, is shorter than the ANPS 2.4, and should only take you 3 to 4 minutes to complete. For psychologists interested in psychometric properties of the ANPS-AR, we refer you to our scientific paper published in *Personality Neuroscience* (Montag and Davis 2018). Clearly, the ANPS-AR and the ANPS 2.4 might undergo further changes in the future to improve their already acceptable reliability and validity.

In the following, we ask you to rate yourself on the adjectives presented. We ask you to rate how you see yourself with respect to each item in general. Alongside each item, you will see listed which primary emotional system is being assessed (the middle column of the following Table A.1). Add the points for each scale and sum them up. You can fill in your score in the appropriate field below. Given some slight to larger differences in primary emotional systems depending on gender, we present two different options with which to compare your data set. In Table A.2 you will find the reference scores for males, and in Table A.3 you will find the reference scores for females. In our sample, only very small correlations between primary emotional systems and age appeared. Therefore, we present the data without further splitting the tables into different age groups.

The comparison data represents a subsample of a large-scale investigation, in which study participants filled in questionnaires on a website in order to get information about their *Gaming Disorder* scores (see also Chapter 5). Therefore, this website might have attracted only people interested in gaming. If gamers or Internet users differ in primary emotional systems from other populations, the data available here would be prone to bias. For example, in other data sets one might expect higher CARE scores in females compared to males. Moreover, the skewed distribution of SEEKING, CARE, and PLAY data (not depicted) hints towards higher scores in this sample than one might expect. This said, the data set available has been drawn from a larger population, with the aim of having an equal number of males and females (much more males were visiting the Gaming Disorder platform). Despite these limitations, we believe that the data available here gives you a rough idea of how your emotional personality compares to others.

A final and very important note: personality is neither good nor bad per se. We have mentioned that such an evaluation depends on many variables, including the niche you are operating in. Ergo, please see the self-assessment as a fun activity to assess your emotional personality. It is not meant to diagnose you in any way or to make you feel bad if your scores differ to a greater or lesser extent as compared to the available data set.

Please read each adjective and answer on the right side how well it describes you in general.	Primary emotional system	Your scores						
		very inaccurate	inaccurate	slightly inaccurate	neither	slightly accurate	accurate	very accurate
purposeful	SEEKING +	1	2	3	4	5	6	7
anxious	FEAR +	1	2	3	4	5	6	7
caring	CARE +	1	2	3	4	5	6	7
hot-headed	ANGER +	1	2	3	4	5	6	7
funny	PLAY +	1	2	3	4	5	6	7
often sad	SADNESS +	1	2	3	4	5	6	7
unimaginative	SEEKING −	7	6	5	4	3	2	1
nervous	FEAR +	1	2	3	4	5	6	7
unsympathetic	CARE −	7	6	5	4	3	2	1
aggressive	ANGER +	1	2	3	4	5	6	7
not playful	PLAY −	7	6	5	4	3	2	1
socially insecure	SADNESS +	1	2	3	4	5	6	7
dynamic	SEEKING +	1	2	3	4	5	6	7
relaxed	FEAR −	7	6	5	4	3	2	1
nurturing	CARE +	1	2	3	4	5	6	7
not argumentative	ANGER −	7	6	5	4	3	2	1
jokes around	PLAY +	1	2	3	4	5	6	7
socially confident	SADNESS −	7	6	5	4	3	2	1
curious	SEEKING +	1	2	3	4	5	6	7
a worrier	FEAR +	1	2	3	4	5	6	7
warm	CARE +	1	2	3	4	5	6	7

temperamental	ANGER +	1	2	3	4	5	6	7
humorous	PLAY +	1	2	3	4	5	6	7
sensitive to rejection	SADNESS +	1	2	3	4	5	6	7

Table A.1: Rate your emotional personality.

	Your score	Mean-Sum score	Standard deviation
SEEKING		24.95	2.53
FEAR		13.85	5.87
CARE		21.74	4.11
ANGER		15.03	5.20
PLAY		23.34	4.02
SADNESS		13.24	5.83

Table A.2: Male data set for comparison (1,942 participants; mean age: 26.77 (standard deviation: 7.04); please note that the standard deviation offers insights into how the scores scatter around the mean, hence how homogenously the scores cluster around the mean).

	Your score	Mean-Sum score	Standard deviation
SEEKING		22.27	2.82
FEAR		17.93	5.43
CARE		21.34	4.01
ANGER		15.21	4.97
PLAY		21.42	4.14
SADNESS		17.51	5.42

Table A.3: Female data set for comparison (2,107 participants; mean age: 26.98 (standard deviation: 7.45); please note that the standard deviation offers insight into how the scores scatter around the mean, hence how homogenously the scores cluster around the mean).

Bibliography

Ackerman, Brian P., Jo Ann A. Abe, and Carroll E. Izard. 1998. "Differential Emotions Theory and Emotional Development." In *What Develops in Emotional Development?*, edited by Michael F. Mascolo and Sharon Griffin, 85–106. Boston: Springer. DOI: 10.1007/978-1-4899-1939-7_4.

Alberini, Cristina M. 2010. "Long-Term Memories: The Good, the Bad, and the Ugly." Cerebrum: The Dana Forum on *Brain Science* 2010 (October). https://www.ncbi.nlm.nih.gov/pmc/articles/PMC3574792/.

Altschul, Drew M., Emma K. Wallace, Ruth Sonnweber, Masaki Tomonaga, and Alexander Weiss. 2017. "Chimpanzee Intellect: Personality, Performance and Motivation with Touchscreen Tasks." *Royal Society Open Science* 4 (5). DOI: 10.1098/rsos.170169.

Areni, Charles S., and David Kim. 1993. "The Influence of Background Music on Shopping Behavior: Classical Versus Top-Forty Music in a Wine Store." *ACR North American Advances*. https:///www.acrwebsite.org/volumes/7467/volumes/v20/NA-20.

Balda, Felix. 2020. "Musikindustrie – Umsatz weltweit 2018." Statista. https://de.statista.com/statistik/daten/studie/182361/umfrage/weltweiter-umsatz-der-musikindustrie-seit-1997/.

Bannister, Scott. 2019. "Distinct Varieties of Aesthetic Chills in Response to Multimedia." *PLOS ONE* 14 (11). DOI: 10.1371/journal.pone.0224974.

————. 2020. "A Vigilance Explanation of Musical Chills? Effects of Loudness and Brightness Manipulations." *Music & Science 3* (January). DOI: 10.1177/2059204320915654.

Barrett, Frederick S., Kevin J. Grimm, Richard W. Robins, Tim Wildschut, Constantine Sedikides, and Petr Janata. 2010. "Music-Evoked Nostalgia: Affect, Memory, and Personality." *Emotion* 10 (3): 390–403. DOI: 10.1037/a0019006.

Barrett, Frederick S., and Petr Janata. 2016. "Neural Responses to Nostalgia-Evoking Music Modeled by Elements of Dynamic Musical Structure and Individual Differences in Affective Traits." *Neuropsychologia* 91 (October): 234–46. DOI: 10.1016/j.neuropsychologia.2016.08.012.

Beatz, Hercules. 2007. "UT-Kid Am Durchdrehen." *YouTube,* February 15. https://www.youtube.com/watch?v=RKSjoZospqo.

Bernatzky, Guenther, Michaela Presch, Mary Anderson, and Jaak Panksepp. 2011. "Emotional Foundations of Music as a Non-Pharmacological Pain Management Tool in Modern Medicine." *Neuroscience & Biobehavioral Reviews* 35 (9) "Pioneering Research in Affective Neuroscience: Celebrating the Work of Dr. Jaak Panksep": 1989–99. DOI: 10.1016/j.neubiorev.2011.06.005.

Bewernick, Bettina H., Sarah Kayser, Sabrina M. Gippert, Christina Switala, Volker A. Coenen, and Thomas E. Schlaepfer. 2017. "Deep Brain Stimulation to the Medial Forebrain Bundle for Depression – Long-Term Outcomes and a Novel Data Analysis Strategy." *Brain Stimulation* 10 (3): 664–71. DOI: 10.1016/j.brs.2017.01.581.

Billig, Aubrielle. 2016. "New Jersey Proposes 'No Texting While Walking' Law." *Small Business Trends.* https://smallbiztrends.com/2016/04/new-jersey-no-texting-walking.html.

Bleidorn, Wiebke, Christopher J. Hopwood, and Richard E. Lucas. 2018. "Life Events and Personality Trait Change." *Journal of Personality* 86 (1): 83–96. DOI: 10.1111/jopy.12286.

Bolton, Doug. 2016. "The Reason Steve Jobs Didn't Let His Children Use an iPad." *The Independent.* February 24. http://www.independent.co.uk/life-style/gadgets-and-tech/news/steve-jobs-apple-ipad-children-technology-birthday-a6893216.html.

Burgdorf, Jeffrey, Jaak Panksepp, and Joseph R. Moskal. 2011. "Frequency-Modulated 50kHz Ultrasonic Vocalizations: A Tool for Uncovering the Molecular Substrates of Positive Affect." *Neuroscience & Biobehavioral Reviews* 35 (9) "Pioneering Research in Affective Neuroscience: Celebrating the Work of Dr. Jaak Panksepp": 1831–36. DOI: 10.1016/j.neubiorev.2010.11.011.

Caruana, Fausto, Pietro Avanzini, Veronica Pelliccia, Valeria Mariani, Flavia Zauli, Ivana Sartori, Maria Del Vecchio, Giorgio Lo Russo, and Giacomo Rizzolatti. 2020. "Mirroring Other's Laughter. Cingulate, Opercular and Temporal Contributions to Laughter Expression and Observation." *Cortex* 128 (July): 35–48. DOI: 10.1016/j.cortex.2020.02.023.

Chamorro-Premuzic, Tomas, Patrick Fagan, and Adrian Furnham. 2010. "Personality and Uses of Music as Predictors of Preferences for Music Consensually Classified as Happy, Sad, Complex, and Social." *Psychology of Aesthetics, Creativity, and the Arts* 4 (4): 205–13. DOI: 10.1037/a0019210.

Chamorro-Premuzic, Tomas, and Adrian Furnham. 2007. "Personality and Music: Can Traits Explain How People Use Music in Everyday Life?" *British Journal of Psychology* 98 (2): 175–85. DOI: 10.1348/000712606X111177.

Clark, Jenna, Sara Algoe, and Melanie Green. 2017. "Social Network Sites and Well-Being: The Role of Social Connection." *Current Directions in Psychological Science* 27 (December): DOI: 10.1177/0963721417730833.

Coenen, Volker A., Thomas E. Schlaepfer, Burkhard Maedler, and Jaak Panksepp. 2011. "Cross-Species Affective Functions of the Medial Forebrain Bundle – Implications for the Treatment of Affective Pain and Depression in Humans." *Neuroscience & Biobehavioral Reviews* 35 (9) "Pioneering Research in Affective Neuroscience: Celebrating the Work of Dr. Jaak Panksepp": 1971–81. DOI: 10.1016/j.neubiorev.2010.12.009.

Csikszentmihalyi, Mihaly. 2008. *Flow: The Psychology of Optimal Experience.* New York: Harper Perennial Modern Classics.

Darwin, Charles. 1958. *The Autobiography of Charles Darwin.* Edited by Nora Barlow. London: Collins.

Davis, Kenneth L., and Jaak Panksepp. 2011. "The Brain's Emotional Foundations of Human Personality and the Affective Neuroscience Personality Scales." *Neuroscience & Biobehavioral Reviews* 35 (9) "Pioneering Research in Affective Neuroscience: Celebrating the Work of Dr. Jaak Panksepp": 1946–58. DOI: 10.1016/j.neubiorev.2011.04.004.

Davis, Kenneth L., Jaak Panksepp, and Larry Normansell. 2003. "The Affective Neuroscience Personality Scales: Normative Data and Implications." *Neuropsychoanalysis* 5 (1): 57–69. DOI: 10.1080/15294145.2003.10773410.

Davis, Kenneth L., Jaak Panksepp, and Mark Solms. 2018. *The Emotional Foundations of Personality: A Neurobiological and Evolutionary Approach.* 1st edn. W.W. Norton & Company.

Diener, Ed, Robert A. Emmons, Randy J. Larsen, and Sharon Griffin. 1985. "The Satisfaction with Life Scale." *Journal of Personality Assessment* 49 (1): 71–75. DOI: 10.1207/s15327752jpa4901_13.

Diener, Ed, Christie Scollon, and Richard Lucas. 2003. "The Evolving Concept of Subjective Well-Being: The Multifaceted Nature of Happiness." *Advances in Cell Aging and Gerontology* 15 (December): 187–219. DOI: 10.1016/S1566-3124(03)15007-9.

Donahue, C.J., M.F.Glasser, T.M. Preuss, J.K. Rilling, and D.C. Van Essen. 2018. "Quantitative Assessment of Prefrontal Cortex in Humans Relative to Nonhuman Primates." *Proceedings of the National Academy of Sciences* 115 (22): E5183–E5192. DOI: 10.1073/pnas.1721653115.

Duradoni, Mirko, Federico Innocenti, and Andrea Guazzini. 2020. "Well-Being and Social Media: A Systematic Review of Bergen Addiction Scales." *Future Internet* 12 (2): 24. DOI: 10.3390/fi12020024.

Edmonds, Grant W., Joshua J. Jackson, Jennifer V. Fayard, and Brent W. Roberts. 2008. "Is Character Fate, or Is There

Hope to Change My Personality Yet?" *Social and Personality Psychology Compass* 2 (1): 399–413. DOI: 10.1111/j.1751-9004.2007.00037.x.

Ekman, Paul, and Wallace V. Friesen. 1971. "Constants across Cultures in the Face and Emotion." *Journal of Personality and Social Psychology* 17 (2): 124–29. DOI: 10.1037/h0030377.

Ekman, Paul, Wallace V. Friesen, and Phoebe Ellsworth. 2013. *Emotion in the Human Face: Guidelines for Research and an Integration of Findings.* Burlington: Elsevier.

Ekman, Paul, and Karl G. Heider. 1988. "The Universality of a Contempt Expression: A Replication." *Motivation and Emotion* 12 (3): 303–8. DOI: 10.1007/BF00993116.

Fischer, Agneta, and Roger Giner-Sorolla. 2016. "Contempt: Derogating Others While Keeping Calm." *Emotion Review* 8 (4): 346–57. DOI: 10.1177/1754073915610439.

Fleischer, Lisa. 2018. "Nach 12 Jahren: Das Unreal Tournament Kid beantwortet Fragen zu seinen alten Videos." *GIGA*. 2018. https://www.giga.de/spiele/unreal-tournament/news/nach-12-jahren-das-unreal-tournament-kid-beantwortet-fragen-zu-seinen-alten-videos/.

Florio, M., M. Albert, E. Taverna, T. Namba, H. Brandl, E. Lewitus, C. Haffner, A. Sykes, F. Wong, J. Peters, E. Guhr, S. Klemroth, K. Prufer, J. Kelso, R. Naumann, I. Nusslein, A. Dahl, R. Lachmann, S. Paabo, and W. Huttner. 2015. "Human-specific Gene ARHGAP11B Promotes Basal Progenitor Amplification and Neocortex Expansion." *Science* 347 (6229): 1465–70. DOI: 10.1126/science.aaa1975.

Foer, Jonathan Safran. 2009. *Eating Animals.* New York: Little, Brown and Company.

Fonseca-Azevedo, Karina, and Suzana Herculano-Houzel. 2012. "Metabolic Constraint Imposes Tradeoff between Body Size and Number of Brain Neurons in Human Evolution." *Proceedings of the National Academy of Sciences* 109 (45): 18571–76. DOI: 10.1073/pnas.1206390109.

Gosling, S.D. 2001. "From Mice to Men: What Can We Learn about Personality from Animal Research?" *Psychological Bulletin* 127 (1): 45–86. DOI: 10.1037/0033-2909.127.1.45.

Gosling, Samuel D., Virginia S.Y. Kwan, and Oliver P. John. 2003. "A Dog's Got Personality: A Cross-Species

Comparative Approach to Personality Judgments in Dogs and Humans." *Journal of Personality and Social Psychology* 85 (6): 1161–69. DOI: 10.1037/0022-3514.85.6.1161.

Happy Planet Index. 2016. "How Is the Happy Planet Index Calculated?" https://happyplanetindex.org/about#how.

Hartvig, Nicolai. 2010. "Virtually Addicted: Weaning Koreans off Their Wired World." *CNN,* March 25. http://www.cnn.com/2010/TECH/03/25/online.gaming.addiction/index.html.

"Heimtiermarkt Deutschland." 2019. *Statista.* https://de.statista.com/statistik/studie/id/7127/dokument/haustiere---statista-dossier/.

Henrich, Joseph, Steven J. Heine, and Ara Norenzayan. 2010. "Most People Are Not WEIRD." *Nature* 466 (29). DOI: 10.1038/466029a.

Hoeckner, Berthold, Emma W. Wyatt, Jean Decety, and Howard Nusbaum. 2011. "Film Music Influences How Viewers Relate to Movie Characters." *Psychology of Aesthetics, Creativity, and the Arts* 5 (2): 146–53. DOI: 10.1037/a0021544.

Hunt, Katie, and Naomie Ng. 2015. "Man Dies after 3-Day Internet Gaming Binge." *CNN,* January 19. https://edition.cnn.com/2015/01/19/world/taiwan-gamer-death/.

Huron, David. 2011. "Why Is Sad Music Pleasurable? A Possible Role for Prolactin." *Musicae Scientiae* 15 (July): 146–58. DOI: 10.1177/1029864911401171.

Izard, C. E., and S. Buechler. 1980. "Chapter 7 – ASPECTS OF CONSCIOUSNESS AND PERSONALITY IN TERMS OF DIFFERENTIAL EMOTIONS THEORY." In *Theories of Emotion,* edited by Robert Plutchik and Henry Kellerman, 165–87. Orlando: Academic Press. DOI: 10.1016/B978-0-12-558701-3.50013-2.

Key, Timothy J., Paul N. Appleby, and Magdalena S. Rosell. 2006. "Health Effects of Vegetarian and Vegan Diets." *Proceedings of the Nutrition Society* 65 (1): 35–41. DOI: 10.1079/PNS2005481.

Kahneman, Daniel, and Angus Deaton. 2010. "High Income Improves Evaluation of Life but Not Emotional Well-

Being." *Proceedings of the National Academy of Sciences* 107 (38): 16489–93. DOI: 10.1073/pnas.1011492107.

Knežević, Goran, Ljiljana B. Lazarević, Christian Montag, and Ken Davis. 2020. "Relations Between Lexical and Biological Perspectives on Personality: New Evidence Based on HEXACO and Affective Neuroscience Theory." *Journal of Personality Assessment* 102 (3): 325–36. DOI: 10.1080/00223891.2018.1553782.

Krack, Paul, Rajeev Kumar, Claire Ardouin, Patricia Limousin Dowsey, John M. McVicker, Alim-Louis Benabid, and Pierre Pollak. 2001. "Mirthful Laughter Induced by Subthalamic Nucleus Stimulation." *Movement Disorders* 16 (5): 867–75. DOI: 10.1002/mds.1174.

Kushlev, Kostadin, and Elizabeth W. Dunn. 2015. "Checking Email Less Frequently Reduces Stress." *Computers in Human Behavior* 43 (February): 220–28. DOI: 10.1016/j.chb.2014.11.005.

Kushlev, Kostadin, Elizabeth W. Dunn, and Richard E. Lucas. 2015. "Higher Income Is Associated With Less Daily Sadness but Not More Daily Happiness." *Social Psychological and Personality Science* 6 (5): 483–89. DOI: 10.1177/1948550614568161.

Laajaj, R., K. Macours, D.A.P. Hernandez, O. Arias, S.D. Gosling, J. Potter, and R. Vakis. 2019. "Challenges to Capture the Big Five Personality Traits in non-WEIRD Populations." *Science advances* 5 (7): eaaw5226. DOI: 10.1126/sciadv.aaw5226.

Lachmann, Bernd, Rayna Sariyska, Christopher Kannen, Konrad Błaszkiewicz, Boris Trendafilov, Ionut Andone, Mark Eibes, et al. 2018. "Contributing to Overall Life Satisfaction: Personality Traits Versus Life Satisfaction Variables Revisited – Is Replication Impossible?" *Behavioral Sciences* 8 (1): 1. DOI: 10.3390/bs8010001.

Lachmann, Bernd, Cornelia Sindermann, Rayna Y. Sariyska, Ruixue Luo, Martin C. Melchers, Benjamin Becker, Andrew J. Cooper, and Christian Montag. 2018a. "The Role of Empathy and Life Satisfaction in Internet and Smartphone Use Disorder." *Frontiers in Psychology* 9: 398. DOI: 10.3389/fpsyg.2018.00398/full.

Ladinig, Olivia, Charles Brooks, Niels Chr. Hansen, Katelyn Horn, and David Huron. 2019. "Enjoying Sad Music: A Test of the Prolactin Theory." *Musicae Scientiae.* DOI: 10.1177/1029864919890900.

Laeng, Bruno, Lise Eidet, Unni Sulutvedt, and Jaak Panksepp. 2016. "Music Chills: The Eye Pupil as a Mirror to Music's Soul." *Consciousness and Cognition* 44 (August): 161–78. DOI: 10.1016/j.concog.2016.07.009.

Langer, Emily. 2017. "Jaak Panksepp, 'Rat Tickler' Who Revealed Emotional Lives of Animals, Dies at 73." *Washington Post,* April 21. https://www.washingtonpost. com/national/health-science/jaak-panksepp-rat-tickler-who-revealed-emotional-lives-of-animals-dies-at-73/2017/04/21/01e367ce-2536-11e7-a1b3-faff0034e2de_story. html.

Lyubomirsky, Sonja, and Heidi S. Lepper. 1999. "A Measure of Subjective Happiness: Preliminary Reliability and Construct Validation." *Social Indicators Research* 46 (2): 137–55. DOI: 10.1023/A:1006824100041.

MacLean, P.D. 1990. *The Triune Brain in Evolution: Role in Paleocerebral Functions.* New York: Plenum Press.

Markett, Sebastian, Christian Montag, and Martin Reuter. 2016. "Anxiety and Harm Avoidance." In *Neuroimaging Personality, Social Cognition, and Character,* edited by John R. Absher and Jasmin Cloutier, 91-112. London: Academic Press. DOI: 10.1016/B978-0-12-800935-2.00005-1.

———. 2018. "Network Neuroscience and Personality." *Personality Neuroscience* 1: E14. DOI: 10.1017/pen.2018.12.

Markett, Sebastian, Olga A. Wudarczyk, Bharat B. Biswal, Philippe Jawinski, and Christian Montag. 2018. "Affective Network Neuroscience." *Frontiers in Neuroscience* 12. DOI: 10.3389/fnins.2018.00895.

Martinez, Edecio. 2009. "Game Over For Teen Who Killed Mother over Video Game." *CBS News,* June 17. https:// www.cbsnews.com/news/game-over-for-teen-who-killed-mother-over-video-game/.

Maslow, A. H. 1943. "A Theory of Human Motivation." *Psychological Review* 50 (4): 370–96. DOI: 10.1037/h0054346.

Matsumoto, David, and Paul Ekman. 2004. "The Relationship Among Expressions, Labels, and Descriptions of Contempt." *Journal of Personality and Social Psychology* 87 (4): 529–40. DOI: 10.1037/0022-3514.87.4.529.

McCrae, Robert R. 2007. "Aesthetic Chills as a Universal Marker of Openness to Experience." *Motivation and Emotion* 31 (1): 5–11. DOI: 10.1007/s11031-007-9053-1.

McCrae, Robert R., and Oliver P. John. 1992. "An Introduction to the Five-Factor Model and Its Applications." *Journal of Personality* 60 (2): 175–215. DOI: 10.1111/j.1467-6494.1992.tb00970.x.

Melchers, Martin, Mei Li, Yafei Chen, Wanqi Zhang, and Christian Montag. 2015. "Low Empathy Is Associated with Problematic Use of the Internet: Empirical Evidence from China and Germany." *Asian Journal of Psychiatry* 17 (October): 56–60. DOI: 10.1016/j.ajp.2015.06.019.

Miller, Anesa. 2013. *To Boldly Go: Essays for the Turning Years*. 1st edn. Bowling Green: CreateSpace Independent Publishing Platform.

Mischel, Walter, and Yuichi Shoda. 1995. "A Cognitive-Affective System Theory of Personality: Reconceptualizing Situations, Dispositions, Dynamics, and Invariance in Personality Structure." *Psychological Review* 102 (2): 246–68. DOI: 10.1037/0033-295X.102.2.246.

Mithen, Steven. 2009. "The Music Instinct. The Evolutionary Basis of Musicality." *Annals of the New York Academy of Sciences* 1169: 3–12. DOI: 10.1111/j.1749-6632.2009.04590.x

Mobbs, Dean, Predrag Petrovic, Jennifer L. Marchant, Demis Hassabis, Nikolaus Weiskopf, Ben Seymour, Raymond J. Dolan, and Christopher D. Frith. 2007. "When Fear Is Near: Threat Imminence Elicits Prefrontal-Periaqueductal Gray Shifts in Humans." *Science* 317 (5841): 1079–83. DOI: 10.1126/science.1144298.

Montag, Christian. 2016. *Persönlichkeit – Auf der Suche nach unserer Individualität*. Berlin: Springer-Verlag.

———. 2018. *Homo Digitalis – Smartphones, Soziale Netzwerke und das Gehirn*. Wiesbaden: Springer.

Montag, Christian, and Benjamin Becker. 2019. "Psychological and Neuroscientific Advances to Understand Internet Use

Disorder." *Neuroforum* 25 (2): 99–107. DOI: 10.1515/nf-2018-0026.

Montag, Christian, Benjamin Becker, and Chunmei Gan. 2018. "The Multipurpose Application WeChat: A Review on Recent Research." *Frontiers in Psychology* 9. DOI: 10.3389/fpsyg.2018.02247.

Montag, Christian, Konrad Błaszkiewicz, Rayna Sariyska, Bernd Lachmann, Ionut Andone, Boris Trendafilov, Mark Eibes, and Alexander Markowetz. 2015. "Smartphone Usage in the 21st Century: Who Is Active on WhatsApp?" *BMC Research Notes* 8 (1): 331. DOI: 10.1186/s13104-015-1280-z.

Montag, Christian, and Kenneth L. Davis. 2018. "Affective Neuroscience Theory and Personality: An Update." *Personality Neuroscience* 1 (August). DOI: 10.1017/pen.2018.10.

Montag, Christian, Kenneth L. Davis, Ljiljana B. Lazarevic, and Goran Knezevic. 2019. "A Serbian Version of the ANPS and Its Link to the Five-Factor Model of Personality." *Open Psychology* 1 (1): 303–16. DOI: 10.1515/psych-2018-0019.

Montag, Christian, and Jon D. Elhai. 2019. "A New Agenda for Personality Psychology in the Digital Age?" *Personality and Individual Differences* 147 (September): 128–34. DOI: 10.1016/j.paid.2019.03.045.

Montag, Christian, and Elisabeth Hahn. 2018. "Nature–Nurture Debate." In *Encyclopedia of Personality and Individual Differences,* edited by Virgil Zeigler-Hill and Todd K. Shackelford, 1–5. Cham: Springer International Publishing. DOI: 10.1007/978-3-319-28099-8_822-1.

Montag, Christian, and Jaak Panksepp. 2016. "Primal Emotional-Affective Expressive Foundations of Human Facial Expression." *Motivation and Emotion* 40 (5): 760–66. DOI: 10.1007/s11031-016-9570-x.

———. 2017. "Personality Neuroscience: Why It Is of Importance to Consider Primary Emotional Systems!" In *Encyclopedia of Personality and Individual Differences,* edited by Virgil Zeigler-Hill and Todd K. Shackelford, 1–11. Cham: Springer International Publishing. DOI: 10.1007/978-3-319-28099-8_1338-1.

————. 2017a. "Primary Emotional Systems and Personality: An Evolutionary Perspective." *Frontiers in Psychology* 8. DOI: 10.3389/fpsyg.2017.00464.

Montag, C., M. Reuter, and N. Axmacher. 2011. "How One's Favorite Song Activates the Reward Circuitry of the Brain: Personality Matters!" *Behavioural Brain Research* 225 (2): 511–14. DOI: 10.1016/j.bbr.2011.08.012.

Montag, Christian, Cornelia Sindermann, Benjamin Becker, and Jaak Panksepp. 2016. "An Affective Neuroscience Framework for the Molecular Study of Internet Addiction." *Frontiers in Psychology* 7: 1906. DOI: 10.3389/fpsyg.2016.01906.

Montag, Christian, and Peter Walla. 2016. "Carpe Diem Instead of Losing Your Social Mind: Beyond Digital Addiction and Why We All Suffer from Digital Overuse." *Cogent Psychology* 3 (1). DOI: 10.1080/23311908.2016.1157281

Montag, Christian, Elisa Wegmann, Rayna Sariyska, Zsolt Demetrovics, and Matthias Brand. 2020. "How to Overcome Taxonomical Problems in the Study of Internet Use Disorders and What to Do with 'Smartphone Addiction'?" *Journal of Behavioral Addictions* 1: 1–7. DOI: 10.1556/2006.8.2019.59.

Montag, Christian, Katharina Widenhorn-Müller, Jaak Panksepp, and Markus Kiefer. 2017. "Individual Differences in Affective Neuroscience Personality Scale (ANPS) Primary Emotional Traits and Depressive Tendencies." *Comprehensive Psychiatry* 73 (February): 136–42. DOI: 10.1016/j.comppsych.2016.11.007.

Morton, F., Phyllis Lee, Hannah Buchanan-Smith, Sarah Brosnan, Bernard Thierry, Annika Paukner, Frans Waal, Jane Widness, Jennifer Essler, and Alexander Weiss. 2013. "Personality Structure in Brown Capuchin Monkeys (Sapajus Apella): Comparisons with Chimpanzees (Pan Troglodytes), Orangutans (Pongo Spp.), and Rhesus Macaques (Macaca Mulatta)." *Journal of Comparative Psychology* 127 (August): 282–90. DOI: 10.1037/a0031723.

Mueller, Karsten, Thomas Fritz, Toralf Mildner, Maxi Richter, Katrin Schulze, Jöran Lepsien, Matthias L. Schroeter, and Harald E. Möller. 2015. "Investigating the Dynamics of the

Brain Response to Music: A Central Role of the Ventral Striatum/Nucleus Accumbens." *NeuroImage* 116 (August): 68–79. DOI: 10.1016/j.neuroimage.2015.05.006.

Müller, Kai W., Heide Glaesmer, Elmar Brähler, Klaus Woelfling, and Manfred E. Beutel. 2014. "Prevalence of Internet Addiction in the General Population: Results from a German Population-Based Survey." *Behaviour & Information Technology* 33 (7): 757–66. DOI: 10.1080/0144929X.2013.810778.

Nettle, Daniel. 2006. "The Evolution of Personality Variation in Humans and Other Animals." *The American Psychologist* 61 (October): 622–31. DOI: 10.1037/0003-066X.61.6.622.

———. 2009. *Personality: What Makes You the Way You Are.* Oxford: Oxford University Press.

Nutt, David. 2012. *Drugs without the Hot Air: Making Sense of Legal and Illegal Drugs.* La Vergne: UIT Cambridge Ltd.

Orri, Massimiliano, Alexandra Rouquette, Jean-Baptiste Pingault, Caroline Barry, Catherine Herba, Sylvana M. Côté, and Sylvie Berthoz. 2018. "Longitudinal and Sex Measurement Invariance of the Affective Neuroscience Personality Scales." *Assessment* 25 (5): 653–66. DOI: 10.1177/1073191116656795.

Panksepp, Jaak. 1998. *Affective Neuroscience: The Foundations of Human and Animal Emotions.* New York: Oxford University Press.

———. 2003. "Feeling the Pain of Social Loss." *Science* 302 (5643): 237–39. DOI: 10.1126/science.1091062.

———. 2005. "Affective Consciousness: Core Emotional Feelings in Animals and Humans." *Consciousness and Cognition, Neurobiology of Animal Consciousness* 14 (1): 30–80. DOI: 10.1016/j.concog.2004.10.004.

———. 2006. "Emotional Endophenotypes in Evolutionary Psychiatry." *Progress in Neuro-Psychopharmacology and Biological Psychiatry* 30 (5): 774–84. DOI: 10.1016/j. pnpbp.2006.01.004.

———. 2010. "Affective Neuroscience of the Emotional BrainMind: Evolutionary Perspectives and Implications for Understanding Depression." *Dialogues in Clinical*

Neuroscience 12 (4): 533–45. https://www.ncbi.nlm.nih.gov/pmc/articles/PMC3181986/.

———. 2010a. The Primal Power of Play." *YouTube,* June 16. https://www.youtube.com/watch?v=3KanfLqKXYg.

———. 2014. "The Science of Emotions: Jaak Panksepp at TEDxRainier." *TEDxSeattle.* https://tedxseattle.com/talks/the-science-of-emotions-jaak-panksepp-at-tedxrainier/.

Panksepp, Jaak, and Günther Bernatzky. 2002. "Emotional Sounds and the Brain: The Neuro-Affective Foundations of Musical Appreciation." *Behavioural Processes* 60 (2): 133–55. DOI: 10.1016/S0376-6357(02)00080-3.

Panksepp, Jaak, and Lucy Biven. 2012. *The Archaeology of Mind: Neuroevolutionary Origins of Human Emotions.* 1st edn. New York: W.W. Norton & Company.

Panksepp, Jaak, and Jeffrey Burgdorf. 2000. "50-KHz Chirping (Laughter?) In Response to Conditioned and Unconditioned Tickle-Induced Reward in Rats: Effects of Social Housing and Genetic Variables." *Behavioural Brain Research* 115 (1): 25–38. DOI: 10.1016/S0166-4328(00)00238-2.

Panksepp, Jaak, B. Herman, R. Conner, P. Bishop, and J.P. Scott. 1978. "The Biology of Social Attachments: Opiates Alleviate Separation Distress." *Biological Psychiatry* 13 (5): 607–18.

Panksepp, Jaak, Larry Normansell, James F. Cox, and Stephen M. Siviy. 1994. "Effects of Neonatal Decortication on the Social Play of Juvenile Rats." *Physiology & Behavior* 56 (3): 429–43. DOI: 10.1016/0031-9384(94)90285-2.

Panksepp, Jaak, and Douglas Watt. 2011. "Why Does Depression Hurt? Ancestral Primary-Process Separation-Distress (PANIC/GRIEF) and Diminished Brain Reward (SEEKING) Processes in the Genesis of Depressive Affect." *Psychiatry: Interpersonal and Biological Processes* 74 (1): 5–13. DOI: 10.1521/psyc.2011.74.1.5.

Panova, Tayana, and Xavier Carbonell. 2018. "Is Smartphone Addiction Really an Addiction?" *Journal of Behavioral Addictions* 7 (2): 252–59. DOI: 10.1556/2006.7.2018.49.

Pettijohn, Terry F. 1979. "Attachment and Separation Distress in the Infant Guinea Pig." *Developmental Psychobiology* 12 (1): 73–81. DOI: 10.1002/dev.420120109.

Pettijohn, T.F., T.W. Wong, P.D. Ebert, and J.P. Scott. 1977. "Alleviation of Separation Distress in 3 Breeds of Young Dogs." *Developmental Psychobiology* 10 (4): 373–81. DOI: 10.1002/dev.420100413.

Polderman, T.J., B. Benyamin, C.A. De Leeuw, P.F. Sullivan, A. Van Bochoven, P.M. Visscher, and D. Posthuma. 2015. "Meta-analysis of the Heritability of Human Traits Based on Fifty Years of Twin Studies." *Nature Genetics* 47 (7): 702–9. DOI: 10.1038/ng.3285.

Pontes, Halley M., Bruno Schivinski, Cornelia Sindermann, Mei Li, Benjamin Becker, Min Zhou, and Christian Montag. 2019. "Measurement and Conceptualization of Gaming Disorder According to the World Health Organization Framework: The Development of the Gaming Disorder Test." *International Journal of Mental Health and Addiction* (June). DOI: 10.1007/s11469-019-00088-z.

Przybylski, Andrew K., and Netta Weinstein. 2017. "A Large-Scale Test of the Goldilocks Hypothesis: Quantifying the Relations Between Digital-Screen Use and the Mental Well-Being of Adolescents." *Psychological Science* 28 (2): 204–15. DOI: 10.1177/0956797616678438.

Reuter, Martin, J. Panksepp, N. Schnabel, N. Kellerhoff, Petra Kempel, and J. Hennig. 2005. "Personality and Biological Markers of Creativity." *European Journal of Personality* 19 (March): 83–95. DOI: 10.1002/per.534.

Rumpf, Hans-Jürgen, Christian Meyer, Anja Kreuzer, and Ulrich John. 2011. "Prävalenz der Internetabhängigkeit." https://www.uniulm.de/fileadmin/website_uni_ulm/iui.gesfuermit/PINTA_Bericht_Endfassung.pdf.

Sariyska, Rayna, Sebastian Markett, Bernd Lachmann, and Christian Montag. 2019. "What Does Our Personality Say about Our Dietary Choices? Insights on the Associations Between Dietary Habits, Primary Emotional Systems and the Dark Triad of Personality." *Frontiers in Psychology* 10. DOI: 10.3389/fpsyg.2019.02591.

Sariyska, Rayna, Martin Reuter, Bernd Lachmann, and Christian Montag. 2015. "Attention Deficit/Hyperactivity Disorder Is a Better Predictor for Problematic Internet Use than Depression: Evidence from Germany." *Journal* of *Addiction Research & Therapy* 6 (209): 1–6. DOI: 10.4172/2155-6105.1000209.

Scarr, Sandra, and Kathleen McCartney. 1983. "How People Make Their Own Environments: A Theory of Genotype → Environment Effects." *Child Development* 54 (2): 424–35. DOI: 10.2307/1129703.

Sha, Peng, Rayna Sariyska, René Riedl, Bernd Lachmann, and Christian Montag. 2019. "Linking Internet Communication and Smartphone Use Disorder by Taking a Closer Look at the Facebook and WhatsApp Applications." *Addictive Behaviors Reports* 9 (June): DOI: 10.1016/j.abrep.2018.100148.

Short, Kevin. 2017. "Here Is the Income Level at Which Money Won't Make You Any Happier in Each State." *HuffPost*, December 6. https://www.huffpost.com/entry/map-happiness-benchmark_n_5592194.

Sindermann, Cornelia, Keith M. Kendrick, Benjamin Becker, Mei Li, Shijia Li, and Christian Montag. 2017. "Does Growing up in Urban Compared to Rural Areas Shape Primary Emotional Traits?" *Behavioral Sciences* 7 (3): 60. DOI: 10.3390/bs7030060.

Sindermann, Cornelia, Ruixue Luo, Zhiying Zhao, Qin Li, Mei Li, Keith M. Kendrick, Jaak Panksepp, and Christian Montag. 2018. "High ANGER and Low Agreeableness Predict Vengefulness in German and Chinese Participants." *Personality and Individual Differences* 121 (January): 184–92. DOI: 10.1016/j.paid.2017.09.004.

Sittler, Mareike C., Andrew J. Cooper, and Christian Montag. 2019. "Is Empathy Involved in Our Emotional Response to Music? The Role of the PRL Gene, Empathy, and Arousal in Response to Happy and Sad Music." *Psychomusicology: Music, Mind, and Brain* 29 (1): 10–21. DOI: 10.1037/pmu0000230.

Siviy, Stephen M., Kelly A. Harrison, and Iain S. McGregor. 2006. "Fear, Risk Assessment, and Playfulness in the Juvenile Rat." *Behavioral Neuroscience* 120 (1): 49–59. DOI: 10.1037/0735-7044.120.1.49.

Solms, Mark, and Jaak Panksepp. 2012. "The 'Id' Knows More than the 'Ego' Admits: Neuropsychoanalytic and Primal Consciousness Perspectives on the Interface Between

Affective and Cognitive Neuroscience." *Brain Sciences* 2 (2): 147–75. DOI: 10.3390/brainsci2020147.

Speaking of Research. 2020. *US Statistics.* https://speakingofresearch.com/facts/statistics/.

Statista Research Department. 2017. "Pets in the U.S." *Statista.* 2017. https://www.statista.com/topics/1258/pets/.

Teffer, Kate, and Katerina Semendeferi. 2012. "Human Prefrontal Cortex: Evolution, Development, and Pathology." In *Evolution of the Primate Brain: From Neuron to Behavior,* edited by Michel A. Hofman and Dean Falk, 191–218. Amsterdam: Elsevier.

Tran, Mark. 2010. "Girl Starved to Death While Parents Raised Virtual Child in Online Game." *The Guardian,* March 5. https://www.theguardian.com/world/2010/mar/05/korean-girl-starved-online-game.

Vassos, Evangelos, Carsten B. Pedersen, Robin M. Murray, David A. Collier, and Cathryn M. Lewis. 2012. "Meta-Analysis of the Association of Urbanicity With Schizophrenia." *Schizophrenia Bulletin* 38 (6): 1118–23. DOI: 10.1093/schbul/sbs096.

Wernicke, Jennifer Mei Li, Peng Sha, Min Zhou, Cornelia Sindermann, Benjamin Becker, Keith M. Kendrick, and Christian Montag. 2019. "Individual Differences in Tendencies to Attention-Deficit/Hyperactivity Disorder and Emotionality: Empirical Evidence in Young Healthy Adults from Germany and China." *ADHD Attention Deficit and Hyperactivity Disorders* 11 (2): 167–82. DOI: 10.1007/s12402-018-0266-9.

Westhuizen, Donné van der, and Mark Solms. 2015. "Social Dominance and the Affective Neuroscience Personality Scales." *Consciousness and Cognition* 33 (May): 90–111. DOI: 10.1016/j.concog.2014.12.005.

WHO. 2020. "Depression." January 30. https://www.who.int/news-room/fact-sheets/detail/depression.

Widen, Sherri C., Anita M. Christy, Kristen Hewett, and James A. Russell. 2011. "Do Proposed Facial Expressions of Contempt, Shame, Embarrassment, and Compassion Communicate the Predicted

Emotion?" *Cognition & Emotion* 25 (5): 898–906. DOI: 10.1080/02699931.2010.508270.

Worldometers.info. 2020. "World Population Clock: 7.8 Billion People (2020) – Worldometer." https://www.worldometers. info/world-population/.

Zachar, Peter, and Ralph D. Ellis. 2012. *Categorical versus Dimensional Models of Affect: A Seminar on the Theories of Panksepp and Russell.* Amsterdam: John Benjamins Publishing Company.